Freeing
Your Heart For
Love

A MEMOIR

LORRINE
PATTERSON

AVIVA
PUBLISHING
New York

Freeing Your Heart For Love, A Memoir
Copyright © 2020 by Lorrine Patterson

Aviva Publishing
Lake Placid, NY
(518) 523-1320
www.AvivaPubs.com

All rights reserved, including the right to reproduce this book or portion thereof in any form whatsoever.

Although this book is based on real-life events, names have been changed to protect people's privacy.

For information, address:
Lorrine Patterson
www.freeingyourheartforlove.com

Every attempt has been made to source all quotes properly.

For additional copies or bulk purchases visit:
www.freeingyourheartforlove.com

Editor: Keith Gordon
Cover Design: Kerry Jesberger/Aero Gallerie
Interior Book Layout: Rachel Langaker/Fusion Creative Works
Author Photo Credit: Calvina Nguyen/Calvina Photography

Cataloging-in-Publication Data is on file at the Library of Congress
Print ISBN: 978-1-636180557
eBook ISBN: 978-1-63618-071-7
Library of Congress Control Number: 2020925647

First Edition, 2020

Printed in the United States of America

To my husband, Gary, my children, and my grandchildren.

I am forever grateful for the joy you bring to my heart,
beauty to my world, and love to my life.
I love you with all my heart and soul.

Thank you for loving and supporting me in this journey.

margaret,
Thank you for
your love and
support!! :)
♡

Table of Contents

Prologue

It was just another weekend with Leon. The week prior, he had been hunting online for the next man to join us in the bedroom. I had no words to tell him that I didn't want to do this anymore. We were a married couple who had made a promise to each other when we married to love, respect, and protect each other, and yet Leon's insatiable desires were making me feel anything but that. I felt like I was falling down a deep, dark hole. I couldn't breathe—it was as if I was trying to scream for help, but nothing was coming out. I was determined to make this marriage work for my family and for myself but at what cost? My determination to find self-worth and meaningful love was pushing me further and further into a void that I might never emerge from.

Leon booked a hotel for us to meet the man of choice. It was a Saturday night. Time for me to get ready. I picked out hot-pink patent leather heels with a peep toe. My outfit was a form-fitting black skirt with a low-cut white top that accentuated my breasts. Leon always wanted me to dress sexy for these men so they would be immediately turned on when they entered the room. I wore a soft, sweet perfume. My hair was down in curls. I put on my best earrings, and we headed to the hotel.

I always needed alcohol to make me feel relaxed during these rendezvous. We opened a bottle of wine when we arrived at the hotel. As we waited for the stranger to show up, I tried to put on my best face for Leon. I wanted him to be proud of me. I wanted to make him happy, so I pushed my own happiness aside and did exactly what he told me.

We heard a knock at the door, and there he was—the man I would be giving my body and soul to tonight. Leon invited him in and asked him to sit on the couch next to me. As we got to know each other, Leon asked this man if he thought his wife, me, was beautiful. The man said, "Yes, most definitely." I sat there quietly as this man started to touch my legs. We then started kissing, and Leon said, "Let's move to the bed." This man started to kiss my neck and my breasts while Leon was undressing me. Leon was behind me, kissing the back of my neck while this man was in front of me. We gave this man a condom, and as he started to put it on his erect penis, I lay there in my naked body feeling empty and soulless. I became the girl that I hated—all to please Leon.

In the middle of all of us having sex, Leon got up and walked away. I thought it was to get a drink of water or to rest a bit, but as I looked over at him on the couch, I saw that his face was cloaked in anger. I called him back to the bed, but he shook his head. "No, I'm good right here." As this man and I continued to have sex, Leon kept scowling at us in anger. Finally, the stranger came, and we were done.

Once the man had gotten dressed and left, I asked Leon what was wrong. I didn't understand what had made him so angry. He said, "It looked like you were enjoying him too much." I was confused. "I thought you wanted me to do this. I thought you wanted me to enjoy it." He didn't elaborate on how he was feeling or what his comments meant. He just told me to get ready.

I held back the pain and tears as I got dressed. The shame I felt walking from our room to the car was unbearable—as if I had bathed in dirt. My feet ached with every step I took. My body was lifeless. No soul, and nothing more to give.

Part One

Escaping the Pain

"It doesn't matter where you are coming from.
All that matters is where you are going."

- Brian Tracy

For me, finding true love was like figuring out what kind of eggs I liked. Maybe this is why the movie *Runaway Bride* is one of my all-time favorites—it reminds me of my relationships. Remember the part where Maggie, played by Julia Roberts, tells Ike, played by Richard Gere, what kind of eggs she likes? If you haven't seen the movie, Maggie is a woman who has been engaged to be married three times but ran away from the altar each and every time. She meets Ike, a reporter, and they eventually fall in love, but not before he gives her a hard time about how she likes her eggs. He tells her with the first guy she liked scrambled, with the second guy she liked fried, and the third guy she liked poached, but what she discovers after trying and cooking eggs in every way possible is that she really likes eggs benedict. Being in a relationship with myself and others was like figuring out what kind of eggs I liked for 29 years. I would do anything and everything to feel and be loved. Doing anything and everything almost killed me.

In June 1972, I was born in Guam, a place I have never seen. When I was three months old, my family moved to Hawaii. I would like to say that I was a bouncing baby girl, but my life would show me otherwise. I don't recall any of my childhood before the age of twelve. I only know what I've been told about my childhood, which is not much. My parents divorced when I was young. They shared custody of me, my three sisters, and my brother, but I lived mostly with my dad up until I was fourteen. My dad was in the Army and was stationed in Hawaii for most of my childhood. We lived on an Army housing base in Hawaii, which everyone called "The Crater." It was located in an inactive crater, and I thought that was the coolest thing when I was young. I made good friends and loved playing outside and exploring the island. The smell of the plumeria trees and tropical air always made me happy. I learned a lot about the Hawaiian culture at school.

I also learned how to play the ukulele and dance the hula. One might think that this was the best childhood, but what lurked behind our front door was a different story. I remember my dad always being in great shape. He worked out and was very active. He ran marathons and played in golf tournaments. He was quite good at both, and he always won trophies and medals. On the exterior, he looked like the greatest dad, but inside, he was an angry and abusive man.

I don't know for certain why he was so angry, but I am guessing it is because he and my mom divorced, and she left him with the children. Or was it because he didn't want to raise us? I always knew when my dad was having a bad day. Sometimes he would warn us, but other times, we didn't know what to expect. A vein popped out of his head when he would yell, and whenever he puffed out his cheeks, we knew that whatever came next would be even more intense. The brown leather belt my dad wore became the beating implement of choice. I could almost hear it when he pulled it from his belt loops. When I knew that I was going to get spanked with my dad's belt, I would put on three pairs of jeans to help with the stinging. It didn't help. I still had the welts and felt the sting. I still don't know why my dad used that belt or yelled at us. I was a good kid and I obeyed all the rules—but I guess obeying all the rules and being a good kid didn't earn me anything.

At the age of fourteen, I moved in with my mom and stepdad. I lived in a small townhouse near the high school that I attended. I hated high school, mostly because I had only a few friends and had the most awkward body. My hair was frizzy and I couldn't ever get it to do anything. I was always jealous of my sisters because they all had nice hair. My mother was a beautiful, controlling, abusive perfectionist. How could someone so beautiful be so unloving? She rarely hit us, but the abuse was very persistent and very mental. She was such a perfectionist that she would wake me at 5 a.m. to braid her hair before work, and if I braided it crooked, she would make me take it out and do it over until it was straight. This behavior would make me feel like I wasn't good enough. She didn't just make me do it all over again, but she would also use a demeaning tone with me. I could barely keep my eyes open so early in the morning, let alone create a straight braid.

My first memory of my mother's controlling behavior was when I got my first job at Denny's as a hostess. My mother convinced me to start working at a young age because she said it would help me later on in life. She was a waitress at Denny's and was able to get me a job. I worked there on the weekends, and I felt excited to be making my own money. I thought I was getting this job to have spending money, but my mother had her own plans for my paycheck. When I got paid, she took every dime. The excitement of making my own money turned quickly to sadness and despair. She always claimed that the money was going to buy me nice things, but I didn't have nice things. I never saw any of my money. This was the beginning of the financial struggles I dealt with in my teen years through adulthood. I was never taught how to manage money and had the mindset that we were always tight on money. The carelessness of spending everything I earned forced me to file for bankruptcy several times throughout my life.

My stepdad, Lawrence, was not a nice man. He did not like me or my siblings, so he always treated us like we were a nuisance. We never knew why he didn't like us. I suspect it was because we were not his birth children, but we would never know. I have lots of memories of Lawrence, but one particularly vivid and very disturbing one is from the day he offered to hem my pants because they were too long. He asked me to try the pants on so that he could see how much he had to hem. While I was standing there, he asked me if the pants fit "up there" and touched me in my vagina area. At the time, I didn't know if it was wrong for men to touch me there—but because I was so young and no one had educated me on what was right and wrong, I didn't know what to think or how to feel. All I knew was that it *felt* wrong.

When I told my mother later that night, she didn't believe me. It was the worst feeling. I didn't understand why my mother would think I was making it up. Later in life, I found out that Lawrence had molested his daughters. Now it all made sense why he never got to see them, and I was able to get my closure on what almost happened to me.

One of the best memories going to high school was meeting my first boyfriend at fifteen. He was my first love—the *only* love I knew at that age. But was it love? I only knew what love was from the movies and what I saw in magazines. His name was Vincent. I met him through my sister's best friend, Allie. My whole world revolved around Vincent. I was so in love. I worshiped the ground he walked on and gave him all of me, even my virginity. I had this princess fantasy that we were going to be together forever. I went to all his football games and wrestling matches. I was his biggest fan. I soon became close to his entire family. He also came from a big family with two brothers and two sisters. His dad was always nice to me. His mom took a while to warm up to me, but eventually, she grew to love me, too.

We were together for a year before my whole world came crashing down. I discovered he was cheating on me with a cheerleader. I can still remember her name to this day. It was truly the saddest day of my life. I lost my everything—the only love that I had in my life, and I couldn't understand what I had done wrong. What was wrong with me? Why didn't he want me anymore? I was so confused how someone could say they love you and then take it away in the blink of an eye. I didn't know where these feelings of unworthiness were coming from—nor did I know that one day they would later destroy my soul.

Shortly after we broke up, my best friend introduced me to her boyfriend's friend, George. I wanted the pain of losing Vincent to subside, so I decided to start dating George. I think this helped with the heartache and pain. George was four years older than me, and I remember feeling excited to date an older guy who was out of high school. He was charming, cute, and he drove a nice car. He seemed very independent and strong, and he definitely had this bad-boy personality. This would get me into trouble later, but he had all the qualities that would make a girl fall in love.

It wasn't long after I met George when my mom and stepdad decided to move to another city. This was very tough on me because I was forced to leave behind my best friend and boyfriend. Despite the distance, George and I continued to keep in touch and he even came to visit me once in a while. I hated the new city I lived in; I had no friends and felt alone. My mom was not supportive of my feelings and always dismissed me when I would try to talk to her about how I felt. She cared much more about whether I was doing the household chores properly.

I was often responsible for cleaning the kitchen floor and bathrooms, and I can still remember when my mom would check my work after I had finished. She would get down on her knees and run her hand across the kitchen floor, particularly underneath the cabinets. If she found a crumb or debris, I would have to clean it all over again. I didn't understand what she was feeling underneath those cabinets, because when I would clean the floor again, I wouldn't find a single speck.

This was her perfectionist behavior, and it was something that I had grown accustomed to. She was never satisfied. When she got angry at me, her yelling not only pierced my soul with fear but also drove the pain deep into my heart. The worst part of her anger towards me was when she would pinch the inside of my thighs and twist until it left a mark. Have you ever been pinched there? It hurts like hell. If my mom wasn't angry and or wasn't yelling, life wasn't normal.

My feelings of depression started to grow stronger and stronger by the day. I felt like there was nowhere to go and no one to turn to. I didn't understand what was happening to me. I didn't understand why I was so unhappy. My support system was broken and non-existent. I lived in a house full of siblings and had a mom, but no one talked to each other about anything—and we certainly never talked about our emotions that lay beneath the surface. For the most part, my siblings and I got along and fought like children do. I can't recall if my siblings felt the same way that I did since we never talked about our feelings to each other. We all pretended to be happy, but deep down I could sense that I wasn't the only one who was sad. I remember the first time I felt like taking my life.

It was 1988. I was sixteen years old. It was a nice summer night and the stars were shining so bright. I was sitting outside on the patio and looking up at the stars. Although I was surrounded with beauty, inside I was broken and sad. I kept saying to myself, "I wish I was dead." I was begging the sky to let me die so that I didn't have to feel so much pain in my heart. I kept trying to think of ways I could take my life. Then I remembered learning in Catholic church as a young girl that a person should never take their own life. I learned that suicide was considered a grave offense and one of the elements that constitute a mortal sin. I always wanted to do the right thing as a young girl and didn't want to commit a sin. I didn't take my own life that night, but the feelings of suicide didn't go away. Years later, these feelings would come back more intense than ever.

That night, I called my boyfriend George and told him that I needed to get far away from my mom. I wanted to escape the unloving home that I lived in, but in reality, I was escaping my depression. He agreed to pick me up the next day and let me stay with him at his place. I didn't tell my mom—I planned to leave without a word.

The next day, I was filled with anxiety and nervousness. In my head, I kept telling myself, "Is this really going to happen? Am I really going to go through with leaving forever? What will my mom do? Will she be sad or look for me?"

Despite all my nerves and feelings, I followed through with my escape. It was one of the hottest days of the summer, and the air was so dry you would sweat as soon as you came out of the shower. I packed my bags that morning and waited for him to call me. When I received the call, I was still very nervous. We both decided that he would pick me up somewhere other than my house so that no one saw him. He told me where he was and asked me to meet him there. I went into my bedroom and closed the door so that my sisters and brother would not hear me. I gathered my packed bags and threw them out the window. Then with all my courage and will, I climbed out after them. I picked up my bags from the lawn and started to walk down the street. The heat was so intense, and the sweat was dripping down my forehead and body. The walk to George was not that long, but it felt like an eternity trying to reach him. I remember feeling embarrassed while walking down the side of the street. Cars were passing by me and staring. I must have looked strange. I was a young, skinny girl carrying two bags down the side of the street. I felt like a fool, and I was worried that someone would report me to the police. I finally reached George and was relieved to see him waiting for me in the parking lot. I got into the car and we took off faster than you could say, "Bye!" We had no plan and nowhere to go. All I knew is that I was out of my unloving, abusive home. Life was going to be good now.

For the next three months, George and I lived with his friends. Almost every night, we slept at a different friend's house. We slept on floors and in cars, but once in a while, we would get a nice warm bed. I felt so happy and didn't want to go home—but I knew school would be starting soon and I wanted to finish high school. I know what you're thinking—how could someone who ran away be responsible enough to go back to school? I always wanted a good career and I knew that education was a huge part of that. I talked to George and we both agreed that I should go back home to finish high school. We had a plan that after I finished high school, I would come back and live with him. The plan we made seemed to be the perfect plan for my life after high school. I would finish high school, turn eighteen, and have every right to live on my own, finally free of the toxic environment. This decision would later be disastrous. At the end of summer, George drove me back home with a new puppy. He wanted to buy me a dog so that I wouldn't miss him as much. We named the puppy Outlaw, but I didn't exactly choose that name—George chose that name, and little did I know it was from a gangster movie that George liked. This should have been my first sign about the type of person George was, but I liked the bad boy in him. I was so happy that I had a puppy, and I didn't care about the name. He was the cutest puppy, and I was in love.

The drive home felt like a long, endless road to nowhere. My anxiety started to kick in. I knew my mom was going to be very upset with me for running away. I was afraid of what was going to happen once I arrived on the doorstep. After hours of driving, we finally reached my house where we were greeted by my mom and stepdad. To my surprise, my mom wasn't upset. Instead, we were met with tears of joy. She told me that she had been so worried about me, and had even contacted the police to look for me. She was beyond happy that I was back home, but she wasn't happy that I brought back a puppy. She was never an animal lover, but despite her concerns, she accepted the situation and allowed me to keep Outlaw. (My mom would later get rid of the puppy by driving out to the middle of nowhere and abandoning him. She brought me and my brother along, and to this very day, I'm still not sure why she would do something so unloving. I still remember my brother and me in the backseat of the car as my mom drove away. We both loved that puppy so much and had gotten attached. We watched the puppy sit there on the side of the road, and I will never forget Outlaw's eyes. They were sad and confused, just like my heart.)

My stepdad had his own feelings about my return, and he wasn't so happy that I was back home. While I was inside catching up with my mom, my stepdad decided to talk with George. My curiosity was killing me because they were talking for so long. When they were finally done, I asked George, "What did he talk to you about?"

He said, "Your stepdad wants me to marry you. He feels that this is the best thing for you and that I should marry you right away."

I couldn't believe my ears. I was only seventeen and wasn't ready to marry. I was at a complete loss. Why would my stepdad try to get rid of me after I just got back home? Why would he force George to marry me? I was so young and had my entire life ahead of me. Later that night, I talked to my mom about it, and surprise! She agreed with my stepdad.

So many thoughts went through my head that night. Why would my mom want to get rid of me when I'd just come back home? Why didn't my mom want me? I was just a kid, and I needed my mom's guidance and support. The familiar feeling of abandonment had surfaced once again. Then I had a thought: this would be my chance to get away from this house for good. After a week of going back and forth, I decided to marry George.

Self-Love Lesson:

"To be beautiful means to be yourself. You don't need to be accepted by others. You need to accept yourself. When you are born a lotus flower, be a beautiful lotus flower, don't try to be a magnolia flower. If you crave acceptance and recognition and try to change yourself to fit what other people want you to be, you will suffer all your life. True happiness and true power lie in understanding yourself, accepting yourself, having confidence in yourself."

- Thich Nhat Hang

2

Transitioning Into My New Life

"Do not give your past the power to define your future."

- Dhiren Prajapati

We planned for the wedding to take place in January in Las Vegas, Nevada. We selected the date of Friday, January 13. I know . . . Friday the 13th. Second sign of bad luck with this guy, but I ignored it, too. I was never a superstitious person, anyway. I am still not sure why we chose that date, but I think it was because it was the only day George could take time off work. My mom had to sign a consent to allow me to marry George because I was under eighteen. I remember feeling so sad that day. I could not get the feeling of abandonment out of my head. I wished that my mom would put a stop to everything and tell me that I was too young and that I had my entire life ahead of me. I wanted my mom to tell me that she loved me and that I would get all the love I needed from her and my family.

That wish never happened. The wedding day came so fast. I didn't even have the chance to meet George's family. Yes, we married without me meeting his mom, dad, sister, or two brothers. Weird, right? Well, we were never traditional, either. His mom was on vacation in the Philippines and his dad was at home when we got married. I don't know where his siblings were, but they weren't invited to the wedding, either. George thought it was a good idea not to tell his family; instead, he thought that it would be best to meet them after we married. He never gave me a reason why. Me being so naïve at the time, I believed everything he said and trusted that he knew what he was doing.

George and I married as planned and spent our honeymoon in Las Vegas. This was the first time in a long time I felt happiness, even if it was just for a moment. I was finally released from the depressing chains of my mom and stepdad's home, and I was truly on my own. Life was good, and we were going to conquer the world together. My sad and depressing days were over for good. Little did I know that this marriage would take me on a roller-coaster ride and drive me into a deeper depression.

After we celebrated our honeymoon, we returned to what I was going to call home for the next year. We agreed to live with my husband's parents and save money until we could afford to move into our own place. When we arrived at George's parent's house, we were greeted by his dad. It was a very awkward moment for me—this man was my new father-in-law and yet we knew nothing about each other. The moment ended up being sweeter than I expected, however, and we were welcomed with open arms. Whew, one parent down, one more to go. I wasn't able to meet George's mom because she was still in the Philippines. A week later, George's mom was returning home and we decided to pick her up at the airport. When George introduced me as her new daughter-in-law, the look on her face was something I will never forget. It was like she just found out she had a flesh-eating disease. I know, so dramatic, but I will never forget that look. I never felt so embarrassed and humiliated. Why did I agree to marry this man without meeting his parents first?

The ride home felt like an eternity. This was the first time I regretted my decision to marry George. My heart sank as thoughts of my future flashed in front of me. When we finally arrived home., George reassured me that his mom would eventually love me. I just needed to give it some time. But in the meantime, I had to endure his mom and aunt talking about me negatively almost daily. Any time I would try to talk to George about it, he would tell me that it was probably just my imagination and not to worry about it.

I decided to focus on finishing high school and not on his mom's feelings about me. The plan was always to finish high school, so I enrolled myself because my mom signed away her parental rights. It felt pretty cool to be on my own. George was determined to provide for me, and he had a lot of ideas about how he was going to do this. One of his big ideas was to start an electropolishing business. He had connections in the industry and was going to start a business with a partner. The business was very successful. We had an abundance of customers, and we were making really good money. Over $100k per year. In the '80s, this was a lot of money!

Not long after the business started, I found out I was pregnant with our first child. We were over-the-moon happy. Remember that my mother-in-law didn't like me? Well, having a child was the best thing that could have happened to our relationship. We grew close and she eventually learned to love me. But as I got closer to my due date, I started feeling scared. I was only 18 years old—what did I know about raising children? Absolutely nothing. I had no parents to support me and give me guidance. I had my mother-in-law, but I wished that my mom was around to share this experience. How was I going to finish high school while I was pregnant? I felt embarrassed and ashamed going to school with a very large pregnant belly. After a lot of thought and determination, I decided to finish high school by doing independent study. This was an alternative to classroom instruction that was consistent with a school district's course of study. With this program, I was able to complete high school and receive my diploma without setting foot in a classroom.

My pregnancy was good for the most part. I didn't develop any health issues, and I ate really well. George was always a good cook, and he cooked for us almost every night (unless his parents were cooking). I loved eating Filipino food. Home-cooked meals were always something I enjoyed with George and his family. It was the one time we could all bond together, and it gave his family a chance to get to know me better. After all, I was the newbie in the family, and no one knew anything about me.

The anticipation of waiting for our son to be born was over. I went into labor in the morning. My water broke at home and my body started to shake profusely because I thought the baby was going to fall out of my vagina. We called the doctor and they said it only meant the baby was coming soon. But they did tell us to get to the hospital as soon as possible, so we grabbed our overnight bag and headed out. I don't know why I thought I would be giving birth as soon as we arrived at the hospital. . . I probably watched a fast birth in a movie or something! In reality, I was in labor for sixteen long, grueling hours. It wasn't a nice sixteen hours until after I got the epidural. After receiving the epidural, I was so exhausted that I slept until I was dilated and had to start pushing. I thought the worse was over and now all I had to do was wake up and push. Boy, was I wrong. Pushing the baby out was another hurdle I had to cross, and it felt like I was running a marathon without a finish line. I pushed for what felt like days. I don't even recall how long I pushed, but I do remember how swollen and sore I was down there. Let's not forget what felt like golf-ball size hemorrhoids that I got from all the intense pushing I had to do. Finally, after sixteen hours of labor and pushing like tomorrow would never come, our baby boy was born.

If you think this was the happy ending to an incredible birth story, it wasn't. My birth experience happened to involve a bunch of interns who were watching the doctor. As I lay there spread-eagle with my entire vagina for everyone to see, the doctor proceeded to stitch me up. You see, I pushed so hard that I tore. I didn't even know such a thing existed until it happened to me. Regardless of the circus that was going on around me, I couldn't have been happier. Junior was born in October 1989, a healthy, beautiful, handsome boy. It was truly the happiest day of our lives, and I wouldn't change a thing despite all the pain. Seeing my baby boy's face and holding him for the first time was a moment I will never forget. I didn't know what was to come with parenting, but I knew one thing: I loved this beautiful, precious human life we created.

We were in the hospital for a day until we were released to go home. Going home brought on a lot of anxiety for me. I couldn't shake that feeling that I now had the responsibility of being someone's mother and raising a child. I was eighteen years old and I hadn't gotten a chance to explore the world yet. I didn't have a career, and I hadn't gone to college. I wasn't even old enough to drink. What business did I have raising a child? Would I be a good mother? Would I be like *my* mother? That thought absolutely terrified me. I tried to erase those thoughts out of my head, but I couldn't. My mind was moving like a hamster running on a wheel. Despite all of my anxiety and feelings of despair, I accepted the responsibility and told myself I was going to figure it out. I promised myself that I would be the best mother I could be regardless of how I was feeling.

The first few weeks after giving birth to Junior were really hard for me. My body was going through a lot of changes and trying to go back to normal after having a baby. Whatever *normal* was. I decided not to breastfeed after unsuccessfully attempting to do it several times. Yes, you can fail at this. I should have studied how to breastfeed. It is an art and nowhere near as easy as you think. There are many things that need to take place to breastfeed: the baby has to latch onto the nipple, and then you have to get used to the pain of the baby suckling. If you're not used to this, it feels very strange. It didn't come naturally to me. I guess some women don't have pain, but my experience was different. I felt *everything*, and my nipples were starting to crack and bleed. My breasts were very painful and hard as a rock, which made it even more challenging to breastfeed. Apparently, if you don't breastfeed, the milk in your breasts has nowhere to go. I tried pumping to relieve the pressure, but nothing provided relief. I ended up getting a breast infection called mastitis, which can typically occur after delivery. After I got the breast infection, the decision to not breastfeed came very easy, and a week out of the hospital, I stopped breastfeeding.

On top of feeling like a breastfeeding failure, I was starting to get depressed. The doctors called it postpartum depression, but was it postpartum if I was already depressed prior to having a baby? A few weeks after Junior was born, he started to cry a lot, but for some odd reason, it was only at night. Nothing would calm him down or make him stop crying. The doctors thought it was the formula we were feeding him, and they suggested that maybe he was allergic to dairy. We changed the formula to a soy-based formula, but it didn't help. We were told that burping him more frequently may help because babies tend to get a lot of gas. Well, that didn't help either. We were out of options and totally sleep-deprived. Finally, the doctor provided us with information about the condition our baby had: colic. This condition is diagnosed when a healthy baby cries or fusses for prolonged periods of time (more than three hours per day). There was no cure for this, and the doctors told us that Junior would eventually grow out of it.

We decided if we were going to have to deal with it, we wanted to find a way to make us all a bit more comfortable. We discovered in our process of figuring it out by trial and error that Junior loved car rides. He would fall asleep in the car and it was the only thing that would make him stop crying. So, what did we do? Of course, we took him on car rides! Car rides were our peace, and sometimes we would drive for hours in the wee hours of the night. Junior would fall asleep in the car, and when we brought him back inside the house, we found that leaving him in the car seat helped us get some sleep. It was a small bit of heaven, and we were willing to take anything—even if it was only for an hour.

George worked a lot, so I was home taking care of our baby alone during the day. At night, if George wasn't working, he was out with his friends at a bar or hanging out with them in our backyard. We always had people over visiting, hanging out, barbecuing, and drinking alcohol. Once in a while, I would get a break and George would care for the baby. It felt so good to finally rest and gather my thoughts. As Junior got older, the grandparents started to help out and babysit him every now and then, and George and I would get a night out on the town together. It felt like we were not parents and had no responsibility—just like when we first met.

It felt good until the drinking became a regular thing. I remember being left in the club parking lot because I blacked out from drinking too much. You see, George wanted to go to the nightclubs almost every weekend. I thought he just loved to dance and listen to music, but his real motivation was one that I would soon discover.

On nights I didn't go with George to the nightclubs, he would go with his friends and come home late—and very drunk. Late one night, I was sleeping and woke up suddenly. I'm not sure what woke me, but when I did, I heard talking in the living room. I went out to find George talking on the phone. I wondered who could he be talking to at 3:00 a.m. I stood in the hallway quietly and listened to his conversation. His voice was soft and flirty. He was complimenting the person on the phone, telling them how sexy they were. At that moment, I knew it wasn't a friend. I started shaking uncontrollably because I was so upset. I wanted to storm into the living room and ask him who he was talking to, but I didn't. I just stood there in the dark hallway silently shaking, distraught and upset.

The next day, I told George that I had heard him on the phone, and I asked him who he was talking to. He told me that I was sleep-walking and it was my imagination. He denied the whole thing and didn't want to talk about it anymore. So, I sat quietly as he dismissed my feelings and what I heard. I buried my feelings into my heart because I didn't want to upset him, and we didn't talk about it again.

Weeks went by and I tried to forget what I heard, but deep down, it was still bothering me. George continued to go out, and he started taking me with him less and less. I remember one night he came home drunk as usual and had a long, white, elegant glove on. It looked like a glove you would see Snow White wearing. He tried telling me that it was his friends and that it was nothing.

By now, the trust I had for George was quickly deteriorating, and my suspicions were confirmed when I found out during a routine pap smear that I had chlamydia. If you don't know what this is, it is a sexually transmitted infection and is spread by having unprotected vaginal, anal, or oral sex. In short, I had an STD. Of course, when I tried talking to George about it, he accused *me* of having an affair. Everything was always my fault, and he took no responsibility for any of his actions. Once again, I sat in silence as I was accused of something I didn't do.

We started to argue a lot more, and my depression was growing worse and worse by the day. I didn't want to be sad anymore, so I mustered up the courage to tell George that I wanted a divorce. He would sweet talk and make me feel special whenever I mentioned the "D" word. He didn't want to split, and he would try everything in his power to make me feel loved. Still being the naïve person that I was, I believed him and stayed. Nothing changed. Everything would be good for a little while, then George would go back to his old ways of disrespecting me: late nights, coming home drunk, and having affairs. He even started to threaten me by saying he would take my car away and kill me if I left him. Pretty soon, everything I felt inside had gone numb. I started to dismiss my feelings and sacrificed my own happiness to stay in the relationship. I didn't want to be the one who broke up the family, and I was terrified to leave.

Self-Love Lesson:

"Remember, you have been criticizing yourself for years and it hasn't worked. Try approving of yourself and see what happens."

- Louise L. Hay

3

My Perfect Secret

"Deep at the center of my being is an infinite well of love."

- Louise Hay

Months went by, and life became routine. I did the same thing every day, feeling like I was trapped in a locked room that I couldn't escape from. I started to focus on finding a career, and thankfully, I landed a really good opportunity with Marriott Residence Inn as a front desk clerk. It was close to my house, but even though the pay was good, I wasn't able to spend the money. George wanted to always be in control of the finances, and he made me put my checks directly into the bank without touching the money. To avoid the argument, I sat in silence and did what he wanted. I felt my soul being torn away from my body and there was nothing I could do about it.

The front desk was a 24 hours/7 days a week operation, so my hours were always different. I wanted to do a good job and I always did what my manager asked of me. This turned out to be a relief—my odd hours kept me away from the house and George, which helped with my feelings of being trapped in a marriage that I didn't want to be in. The only downside was that some nights I wasn't able to tuck my son into bed.

I was doing really well at work and exceeded all expectations of me, and before long, I was offered the position of front desk manager. I happily accepted and was well on my way to an amazing career in the hotel industry. I was a sponge and wanted to learn everything there was to know. I liked the industry so much that I made it a goal to become a general manager of a hotel one day, and I started working towards that goal by taking classes and trainings. After working at the hotel close to my home, I was offered an opportunity to transfer to another location. The location really needed a manager, so I decided to transfer. This would be the best decision I made in my life.

Working and having a career brought me a new sense of purpose. I finally felt like my life was going somewhere and that I was going to be successful in whatever career I landed. But during this time, I was so focused on my career that I didn't pay attention to what was going on in my personal life. It was mostly intentional—I didn't want to face the problems that George and I were having. We talked about going to see a marriage counselor but we never took the steps to actually go.

George's business was still doing well, and life seemed to be getting back to normal. But what was normal? I didn't know what a normal life felt like, so anything was normal to me. We started getting random people coming to our house more frequently. I thought they were there to visit George, but it was more than that. Apparently, my husband had become the neighborhood supplier for "special stuff" that put people into intense, euphoric pleasure. What was this special stuff? I never asked because I knew what the answer would be. I later found out that this "special stuff" was cocaine. He wouldn't tell me the truth, anyway. "Mind your own business," he'd say, "and don't worry about what I am doing."

So I never asked. Instead, I continued to focus on my career goals and raising our son, Junior. But after a while, I started noticing large amounts of cash stashed in George's pants pockets. I didn't ask about how he got the cash, but I guessed it was from the business—maybe he was just keeping it just in case we needed the money? Some nights when he was passed out drunk, I started to take some of the money from his pockets. He never willingly gave me any money, so I had to get creative.

The thought of leaving George was getting stronger as we grew further and further apart. I was becoming a person that I didn't recognize. My life was not my own, and I belonged to a controlling, verbally abusive, lying, cheating husband. By this time, we had been married five years. Wow, where did the time go? Five years just flew by, and I couldn't believe that Junior was going to start kindergarten. I had my own job, and I could support myself and my son now. I thought that I could leave and we would be fine without George.

I finally mustered up the courage to leave George. I waited for him to come home from work to tell him. My nerves were on high alert and my heart was pounding out of my chest. I could literally feel it pumping through my shirt. Fear and anxiety surfaced as I waited for him. It felt like I was waiting for an eternity, then he finally arrived home. I called him into the bedroom so that we could talk. I proceeded to tell him that I hadn't been happy with him and our relationship in a very long time. I informed him that I'd found an apartment and was moving out. His facial expression revealed that he had no idea how unhappy I'd been. As he sat there in silence,

I told him that I wanted a divorce. Surprisingly, he let me leave. And I was free.

Then the moment of weakness happened. We all have those moments when you go back to your ex for the amazing make-up sex. I can't recall exactly how it happened, but I think it was because I was lonely and George was always a charmer. I had a weak moment and let George back into my life and my heart. How could I be that stupid? Yes, I talked negatively to myself, because that was all I knew. In some sick way, it made me feel better to tell myself that I was an idiot. I was sick—I just didn't know it yet. I had worked so hard to get away, and here I was, letting him back in. We ended up having sex one night, and you can guess what happened next. Yep, you guessed it. I was pregnant with our second child. Another boy. I was over the top happy that we were having another baby, and I thought this could be our second chance to make our marriage work. I wanted this baby to bring us back together and help us pick up the broken pieces. I gave up my apartment and moved back in with George.

At first, things seemed better. The whole thing was like a wake-up call for George, and he swore he was finally going to change his behavior for the better. Well, that is what I hoped for, at least. George was focused on his business and I was focused on my career. I didn't stop working because I wanted to make sure that I had a job to go back to after the baby was born.

The day came when our second child was born. Romeo was born in September 1995. It was the most beautiful day, and it was the first time in a very long time that I felt happy and full of joy. Romeo's birth was easy compared to our first child. I was only in labor for six hours and I didn't have any of the symptoms I had with

Junior. Everyone always told me childbirth would get easier after your first child—I had no expectations and was pleasantly surprised. Bringing Romeo home gave me no anxiety this time. I felt like a pro by now, and I felt very proud of what I had accomplished as a young mother—and all of it with little to no guidance.

But it was not all happiness. George and I were still not getting along, and the hope that having a baby would heal our marriage was quickly fading. I felt so alone and depressed. I wanted George to love me so badly that I would sacrifice my own happiness to make him happy. I never brought up divorce again because I didn't want George to get upset. Months and years went by. I didn't know how I was going to leave George now that we had two boys. Then, one day, my first blessing from the Universe appeared—and I didn't even know it. Remember that special stuff George was supplying? Well, it all came crashing down on him.

It was 1997. Junior was eight and Romeo was two. The day started off like it normally did. We did our normal morning routine, with me getting the kids ready for school as George got ready for work. I was at work when I received the phone call. George had been arrested and was in jail. He had been caught with a large amount of a controlled substance in his car. Apparently, he was being followed by law enforcement on suspicion of being a drug dealer.

I can't recall who called me that day, but I remember the feeling that I had—scared but free at the same time. The sentencing for his crime came quickly. I attended with his sister, and for the first time in my life, I saw George look vulnerable and sad. He was wearing an orange jumpsuit with shackles. As much as I wanted to be away from him, I suddenly felt sad as the reality set in. My husband was a criminal, and I would be left to take care of two children and a business by myself. What about my goal of being a general manager at a hotel? Would this dream come true now?

George was arraigned before a judge on charges of possession with intent to deliver cocaine and possession of cocaine. He was found guilty and was sentenced to three years in state prison. When I heard the judge say this, I felt a huge weight lift off my shoulders. It was like my old self was floating out of my body and the new me was taking its place. When the sentencing was over, his sister and I left the courtroom and went to the restroom. His sister was crying as I stood there trying to cry, but no tears fell. As I was washing my hands, I said to myself, "I am free. I am free from the control of George." I felt so happy—it was like I was released from my own internal prison. I finally got my life back, and I was going to live freely, and on my own terms.

The first year of George being gone was very stressful and hard on me and the boys. I was trying to raise two young boys, maintain my dream career, and run the family business that I knew nothing about. Thankfully I had George's family—they were always very generous and helpful in caring for the boys. Every day I worked hard to keep everything running smoothly in our lives. I loved working at the hotel because it kept my mind off of everything that I had to deal with in my personal life. I had one of George's friends helping with running the customer side of the business while I managed the finances. I was still able to keep my hotel job, but I had a hard time focusing on my career. At night, I was lonely and cried myself to sleep. I had no one to talk to or confide in. I cried in silence, and with each passing day, I buried my feelings more and more. I was totally empty inside. My heart was broken, and I felt adrift in my thoughts. I couldn't see past the sadness that I felt inside. I wanted to feel love so badly that it hurt to think about it. I didn't know it back then, but my life was about to change.

One night, I was working a swing shift at the hotel, and I helped a young man with a question he had about the area. His name was Jonathan, and he wasn't from the area. He was looking for a place to eat, and I gave him some recommendations. I thought that was the end of our conversation, but he wanted to talk more, so we did until I had to help other guests. The next day, he came back to the front desk and seemed to be more interested in talking with me than restaurant recommendations. He was cute and charming, with nice hair and a nice smile. He had the most amazing blue eyes I have ever seen. He was also in very good shape. His ethnicity was Irish, which attracted me to him even more. I'd never gone out with a Caucasian man but always wanted to. I think it was the excitement of going out with someone of another ethnicity that excited me. I was smitten each time I saw him at the hotel, and I looked forward to my shift every day. Suddenly work became a lot more than just a career for me. I took a little more time to get ready before work to make sure my hair looked good and my outfit was polished.

Jonathan and I had a lot in common, and I was pleasantly surprised at how well we hit it off. I didn't even know this guy—only that he was in town for business and came very often. He lived in another town a few hours away, and he had a house, a roommate, and one sister. Regardless of what I knew about him, I was instantly attracted to him. He was the first man besides George that I had felt an attraction for. It had been so long since I had felt this way, so long since a man had paid attention to me and wanted to talk with me. I knew it was wrong to feel this way because I was still married to George, but the temptation soon took over my morals. I thought to myself, *George is in jail and he had all those affairs in the past. It is my turn to have some fun.*

Because Jonathon lived in another town, it made the relationship easy to keep a secret. I continued to talk to Jonathan whenever I could, ignoring the feeling of guilt and sin. Jonathan and I eventually exchanged numbers and arranged a time to meet up outside of my work hours. By this time our attraction was so strong that I knew there was no turning back now.

I remember our first sexual experience being awkward for me. George was the only man I had been with for years and years. How would sex with Jonathan be? Would he like my body? I didn't want him to see the stretchmarks on my stomach from having children. Would I be comparing him to George? Why was I thinking about George when our marriage was not working and wanted to feel love again? But these thoughts in my head didn't stop me from doing what my body and mind wanted to do.

Jonathan had nice, warm, big hands that caressed my body in ways that I hadn't felt before. He felt so different inside me than George—a difference that made my body feel out of this world. The way he kissed me felt like soft rose petals on my body. I didn't want the night to end, but I knew that it had to. I had to go back to my life as a mother and a wife to a criminal. The happiness that I was feeling was temporary and disappeared when I left Jonathan.

Jonathan and I managed to see each other every time he came into town for business. When he came into town, I would go to where he was staying because no one could know about him. I didn't want my children or anyone else to know about him. It was my perfect secret, and it would stay that way until we were ready to share it with the world. One night I was in Jonathan's hotel room, and on his dresser, I noticed a small white square item with a clip on it. He was in the restroom and I was curious to see what it was. I opened it up and saw something that appeared to be Japanese writing. I closed it immediately, but I asked him what it was when he came out of the restroom. He was defensive and told me not to touch it. I continued to ask him because I really wanted to know. Was he in some sort of cult? I was raised in a Catholic family, and I was never a religious or spiritual person, so I was very curious to know what it was.

Finally, he decided to tell me and let me into his world. He told me that he was a Buddhist and practiced what they call Nichiren Daishonin Buddhism. My initial reaction was shock. What the heck did this mean? He proceeded to tell me he was born into this practice, as his parents were both practicing when he was born. He told me he was part of an organization called Soka Gakkai International USA (SGI). I was so confused and scared, but I wanted to know more—I had never heard of this type of religion and I seriously thought he was in a cult! This was my naïve self again, uneducated on spirituality and other religions in the world. I asked him more questions, and he educated me. He told that we are all responsible for our own happiness and that the purpose of this religion is to enable human beings to become happy without exception. I said to myself, "Wow! I can practice something that will bring me happiness without exception. What a concept!" I had been seeking happiness for so long. Maybe this was going to help me find this feeling that I had been searching for all my life. All I could think about while driving home was how I could start this practice. I was determined to find out.

A few weeks went by without seeing Jonathan because he didn't have business in town. We still talked on the phone but I missed him a lot. I continued on with my life but I couldn't stop obsessing about being with Jonathan. Around this time, George was finally able to have visitors and he asked me to bring the boys to the prison. At first, I didn't want to subject them to that environment or for them to see their father in prison, but I agreed to do it anyway. Even behind bars, George still had control over me.

The process to see someone in prison was pretty intense. The state prison where George was incarcerated was far from our house, so I had to drive a couple hours away and had to be there at a specific time; otherwise, we would miss the visitation day. Once we arrived, the boys and I had to sit in a waiting area until it was our time to see George. Sometimes it was a quick wait, but other times we ended up waiting for hours. The whole thing was very tough on me and the boys.

When I saw George for the first time in prison, it was a very emotional time for me. He had lost a lot of weight and looked very sad. I don't know why I felt so sad for him after he had treated me so horribly. But seeing the boys always made him happy, and I know it kept him strong while he was in prison. I took the boys to visit him as much as I could, and I ended up going almost every weekend. We talked about the business and how everyone was doing, but it was always surface things and never anything about our marriage and what was going to happen to us. I should have been used to his communication style by now, but I had hoped that being behind bars would have made him more appreciative of us. Even though George being in prison was hard for me as a single mother, I felt my strength and courage growing stronger by the day. I knew that building up this strength and courage would ultimately free me from this toxic relationship once and for all. I needed to be strong for what was to come.

Self-Love Lesson:

"How you love yourself is how you teach others to love you."

- Rupi Kaur

4

Juggling

"For every minute you are angry you lose
sixty seconds of happiness."

- Ralph Waldo Emerson

As the weeks went by, it was getting harder and harder to keep my job at the hotel, manage the business, and raise the boys all at the same time. Finally, the time came and I had to make a difficult decision to end my career at the hotel. It was one of the toughest decisions I have ever had to make—I still had huge dreams of being a general manager of a hotel one day, and more than anything else, I wanted a career to call my own. I made this decision to ensure the best financial support for the family, and the business gave this to us. So I made the decision and left the hotel to focus on managing the business for George until he got out of prison.

Business was still really good because George had built up his clientele prior to leaving for prison, and financially we were doing well, but I still had no idea how to operate an electropolishing business. I wasn't good at managing the money and I started to spend frivolously. I think it was because I never had control over anything and now I was in control. I had an open checkbook with no one to tell me how to write the check! I didn't know what to do with this newfound power, so I went out of control and spent all the money that was coming in.

I was still seeing Jonathan when he came into town every week, and we were getting pretty serious—or as serious as a secret relationship can be. I was still married to George, but I called Jonathan my boyfriend. I couldn't see that, in fact, I was a woman having an affair and Jonathan was my lover. I think it bothered Jonathan that I was married, but he never expressed any issues with it. I wanted to show him how much I loved him, so I bought him things—not just small things, but large investments like remodeling his kitchen and purchasing a BMW motorcycle. I thought if I bought him lavish gifts and did whatever he wanted me to, he would know how much I loved him. All I wanted was to show him how much I wanted to be with him.

Jonathan eventually invited me to his house for the weekends because his business trips were becoming few and far between. You are probably wondering what happened to the weekend visits with the boys and George . . . Well, I decided that I wasn't going to bring the boys to see George anymore, so my weekends became all about Jonathon. Yes, my priorities were all over the place, but all I could think about was spending time with him. I was able to get George's friends or family to bring the boys so I didn't feel as bad for not going. I was over-the-top happy with Jonathan. We got along so well and the chemistry between us was amazing.

I wanted to know more about the Buddhism he was practicing, so he agreed to start taking me to his chapter meetings. Chapter meetings are when you get together with other people practicing in your area. You study, chant, and do a prayer called gongyo. By going to these meetings, I really started to learn and understand what the practice was all about. I met other young women who educated me and taught me how to chant daimoku and do gongyo. I know, what does all this mean? Trust me, it was a foreign language to me, too. It was a Japanese practice and everything was in Japanese. The more I talked to members of the practice, the more I became familiar with what I was doing. Chanting daimoku is saying "nam-myoho-renge-kyo" out loud or silently in front of the Gohonzon.

Let me break it down for you. People tried to explain it to me, but because I was never a spiritual person, I never fully understood it. So, I looked up the definitions for myself. This definition of nam-myoho-renge-kyo is from the website sgi-usa.org:

The essence of Buddhism is the conviction that we each have within us the ability to overcome any problem or difficulty that we may encounter in life. This inherent potential is what we refer to as the Buddha nature, a state of life characterized by limitless courage, wisdom, and compassion. The practice of chanting nam-myoho-renge-kyo aligns the rhythm of our own lives with the world of Buddahood in the universe. It "tunes" our lives, so to speak, so that we can manifest the power of Buddahood in our very beings. To simplify, we awaken to the reality that within our life is unlimited reserves of courage, wisdom, and compassion. Based on this conviction, we can transform any suffering, lead those around us to happiness, and create peace in our communities and the world. The Gohonzon is the scroll that you see in the altar that you set-up in your home. The Gohonzon can literally be translated as "Fundamental Object of Devotion." However, on a deeper level, this object of devotion is revolutionary in that it is meant to serve as a mirror for our own lives. The Gohonzon serves as a blueprint of our lives, it shows us clearly that we possess limitless courage, wisdom and compassion in our present form. As we practice it, we develop faith in ourselves, in our ability to surmount any obstacles or suffering.

Sounds amazing, right? Who doesn't want to be happy and develop the courage and strength to overcome obstacles in your life? I know that I wanted to be happy, so I devoted my life to practicing daily. At first, I was doing it to get close to Jonathan because I thought if I practiced the same faith, he would love me more. The practice did bring us closer in that aspect, but our morals and values when it came to relationships were completely opposite. Jonathan was a ladies' man, and I think I kind of always knew this. To be honest, this was one of the qualities I liked about him! It was that same bad-boy image that attracted me—and would eventually get me into trouble.

When we would attend chapter meetings, certain girls would look at me differently. I would ask him questions like, "Why does this person always look at me this way?" He would tell me that it was all in my head. Sound familiar?

What was really happening was that Jonathan had dated more than a few girls in the practice and there was still some unfinished business. I started to get really suspicious of Jonathan and what he was doing when I wasn't with him.

Around this time, we had planned to spend the weekend together. I was going to come into town on Saturday, but I really wanted to see him so I rearranged my schedule to see him on Friday. My in-laws were able to take care of the boys, so I called Jonathan to give him the good news. I thought he would be just as excited as me, but his response was cold. He told me that he was going out with the guys and that he wasn't going to be home. I said to him, "So, you're not coming back home after going out?" Once again, his response was vague. He proceeded to convince me that it would be best if I just came on Saturday as planned. I was so disappointed and sad that he didn't want to see me. Why didn't he want to see me as much as I wanted to see him?

My feelings of suspicion started to gnaw at me, and I ended up going out with my girlfriends to try and drown my sorrows away with good company and dancing. Girlfriends and dancing always made me feel better. Well, this time it didn't make me feel better—it only made my feelings of insecurity worse. So, what did I do? I drove to his house at 2 a.m. And this wasn't a hop, skip, and a jump, either. He lived two-and-a-half hours away! I shouldn't have been driving at that hour, and especially with the fog coming in. I could barely see the road because the fog was so thick, but I was determined to find out why he was so evasive about seeing me. I had a sick intuition that he was doing something other than what he told me, and I was going to find out if it was the last thing I did.

I arrived at his place around 3:30. His car was in the driveway. As I walked up to his house, I could feel my hands trembling and my heart pounding. What was I going to discover? I knocked on the door and was greeted by his roommate, who wore an expression of shock and surprise.

I said, "Where is Jonathan?"

"He's not here," he answered.

"Where is he?"

"I don't know but let me call him."

He let me inside as he made the call. It was taking more than a few minutes, so I found my way to Jonathan's bedroom. All of our pictures together were removed from his dresser and placed in his drawers. The room was clean and made up like he was expecting company—and that company was not me. His roommate found me and told me that Jonathan was on his way home. As I sat on Jonathan's bed, I was filled with so much emotion and confusion. I knew in my heart that he was out with another girl and that he was planning to bring her back to his room. This emotion and confusion got worse as I waited for him to get home.

Jonathan finally arrived. When he came into the room, I could tell he had been drinking. A lot. I immediately started yelling at him. I demanded to know where he was and why our pictures were in his drawer. He said he was out with his friends and lost track of time. He said that he removed our pictures so he could clean. We continued to argue because I didn't believe a word he said. I knew he was lying. The arguing got so bad that he pulled off his shirt, ran outside, and threatened to hurt himself if I didn't stop questioning him. I still don't know why he removed his shirt, but trying to get the truth out of a drunk person is useless. It was under fifty degrees outside, and I didn't want anything to happen to him, so I sat with him on the cold, wet grass and we cried together. Why was I crying? He was the one who was being dishonest, but I still felt so bad and wanted to comfort him.

The next morning we got up and didn't talk about what happened. It was as if it never happened. We went on with spending the rest of the weekend together. I left on Sunday with a huge hole in my heart. I no longer trusted him. I felt betrayed.

As the weeks went by, Jonathan and I grew further and further apart. The arguing didn't subside—mostly because I didn't trust him regardless of what he told me. The weekend visits were not happening anymore. Why was I so angry with him? I was a married woman and had no right telling Jonathan who to date.

In the end, we both couldn't take the pain, so we decided to break it off. I was heartbroken and depressed. I didn't want to see anything that reminded me of him, so I decided to mail back everything that he bought me along with our pictures together. The package I mailed him was not a pretty, little package. I wanted him to know how hurt I was, so I cut up all of our pictures into small pieces. I took the beautiful gold necklace with a shiny diamond he bought me and damaged it. I cut the necklace into pieces and smashed the diamond, then I put everything into the box and poured super glue over the top of everything. I thought this would make me feel better, but it actually made me feel worse.

I mailed the package, and I called him a few days later to see if he'd received it. His sister answered the phone and told me that he didn't want to talk to me. I demanded to talk to him and she just hung up on me, so I called back and got his father this time. His dad told me the same thing, and he added that I really hurt him by mailing back those items. I didn't care how he felt—all I wanted was some sort of revenge. I guess I got that in the end, but the way I felt inside was the worst pain I had ever felt. I wasn't that person. I loved Jonathan, and we had more good times than bad. I was just so angry and upset at Jonathan for taking my heart and then breaking it. I wanted to be with him forever.

But once the pain subsided, I actually wanted to thank him. He introduced me to the best thing in my life, the Buddhist practice. I would discover years later that this Buddhist practice saved my life, and I now believe that it was the reason I met Jonathan. Unfortunately, this also wasn't the last of my affairs with unavailable men.

It took me months to get over the pain of losing Jonathan. I was so depressed, and I didn't feel like I could talk to anyone about the pain I was feeling. I knew it was bad to hold in all that pain, but I still didn't want anyone to know about him. Deep down, I carried a lot of shame and guilt with me because, here I was, a married woman having an affair while my husband was in prison. What kind of wife does this? At this point in my life, I wasn't practicing Buddhism, and I was trying to keep myself busy with raising the boys and managing the business. The Buddhism reminded me of Jonathan, but I was struggling to find happiness and starting to feel suicidal again. I thought this feeling was gone after that warm summer night at the age of sixteen. It had been eleven years—why was I feeling this again. I wanted to feel happiness so badly, and I remembered what practicing Buddhism could give me, so I reached out to a Buddhist member in the area where I lived. I moved past my feelings of not wanting to practice because of Jonathan—I decided to practice for myself.

She was a very pleasant lady and had a soft voice. She guided me back to the Buddhist practice by chanting gongyo with me. She told me that my suffering could be turned into happiness if I just chanted about it. I thought about what I would chant for, and there were so many things that popped into my head. My immediate thought was that I wanted to be happy and not have this feeling of wanting to take my own life.

I started chanting every day. At first, it was for fifteen minutes, then it turned into thirty minutes, and sometimes an hour. I chanted to be happy and to remove the thoughts of suicide from my head. I chanted with conviction in my heart and repeated in my head over and over that I chose to live my life and be happy. I studied and followed the teachings of Daisaku Ikeda, who was the founding president of the Soka Gakkai. I loved his philosophy of peace: "When we change, the world changes. The key to all change is in our inner transformation—a change in our hearts and minds. This is human revolution."

After picking up my chanting practice, I started feeling better every day, and the pain from breaking up with Jonathan began to subside. I no longer felt angry or hurt. I wasn't practicing Buddhism for him anymore—I was practicing for myself and my own happiness. The thoughts of suicide slowly dissipated, and I no longer had the desire to take my own life. I attended chapter meetings with other members and studied the World Tribune and Living Buddhism, which were two subscriptions that Buddhist members could purchase and study at the chapter meetings. My life finally felt like it was back on track and I was happy again.

It had been over a year since I had seen George in prison. Then out of the blue, I received a call from him. He told me that he was awarded a conjugal visit and wanted me to come see him. If you don't know what a conjugal visit is, it's basically a scheduled period where an inmate is permitted to spend several hours or days in private with a visitor, usually their legal spouses. The parties may engage in sexual activity. When he told me that he wanted to see me, my immediate feeling was that I didn't want to have sex with him. I had already made the decision to divorce him, and this was stronger than ever in my mind. I knew that I no longer wanted to be married to him, and yet he still somehow convinced me to see him.

I agreed with the intention that I was going to tell him that I wanted a divorce. When I arrived at the prison, I went through the normal screening process. It had been so long that I'd forgotten how horrible it was to visit someone in prison. We were shown to a private room where we would spend the weekend. It was like an apartment, only not so warm and welcoming.

George was so happy to see me, but on the other hand, he was not so happy. I didn't wait to tell him what I wanted. I told him right away, "I don't want to have sex with you, and I want a divorce."

He was sitting on the bed and I was standing up. He immediately grabbed me, pulled me close to him, buried his head into my chest, and started to cry. I'd never seen him cry that much in our entire relationship. He told me that he didn't want to lose me and that he was sorry for hurting me all these years. While he was telling me this, I stood there and felt nothing. I was numb to everything he said. I had heard this song and dance many times over, and I knew it was all just an act. It was his way of manipulating me to stay with him, the trick that had always worked in the past. But not this time. Everything he was saying was going in one ear and out the other. I didn't feel sadness while he was crying and begging me to stay. I felt like a cold-hearted bitch—but why did I feel this way? Did he feel bad when I used to cry to him? Did he feel bad for lying and cheating on me our entire marriage? Did he feel bad for making bad decisions and leaving me alone with two young boys to raise?

I told him my mind was made up and I wanted a divorce. He finally agreed, but he asked me to do him one favor: He asked me not to divorce him until he got released from prison. I was confused and asked him why. He said, "If you divorce me, when I am released they will deport me to the Philippines." I thought that was kind of an odd thing to happen, and I didn't really understand it. But for some reason, I trusted his words and agreed to wait until he was released from prison to divorce him. I didn't stay the entire weekend. I saw no reason to stay since there was nothing more to talk about, and I definitely wasn't going to have sex with him.

Despite my decision to divorce George, we kept in touch to discuss the business and the boys. At this point, George's customers were concerned that he might not be released from prison and the poor quality of work being performed by the people helping me was slowly starting to show. We had to decide what we were going to do, and the best decision was to dissolve the business. I contacted an attorney to start processing the paperwork, but it was a very difficult time for me. I didn't know how to dissolve a business or what came along with it. I was worried about how I was going to financially take care of the children. All I knew is that I had to get a job and start working again.

Self- Love Lesson:

"I am a strong believer that fate exists. That everything happens for a reason. That the people we have in our lives are in our lives without accident. There is always meaning. Explainable or unexplainable. There is no such thing as luck. We are all here for a purpose. All we have to do is believe."

- Juansen Dizon

Have you ever reflected back on your life and thought what if I had done things differently? As I reflect back on this part of my life, as hard as it was going through it, I wouldn't change anything. When I met George in 1988, I was a teenager who didn't know anything about parenting or what it was like to be a wife. I was sixteen, and in a dark place of depression and confusion. Growing up, I was never hugged or heard the words "I love you." I wasn't taught how to manage money, and I was always told we didn't have enough. Meeting and marrying George removed me from the toxic environment of my home, and even though it put me into the same type of environment (if not worse), it saved me from the suicidal pit I was in.

In May of 2020, George passed away at the age of 52. Gone too soon. I now know that I had to go through these hard lessons of life with him to become who I am today. I married at the young age of seventeen and became a mother before I graduated high school. I met a guy who I thought was the next love of my life and fell deeply in love with him, only to find out that he was not the one for me. Meeting Jonathon was for one purpose, and that was to be introduced to the beautiful spiritual practice of Nichiren Buddhism. These life lessons have taught me not only how to be strong in extreme situations, but most importantly, how to find forgiveness in my heart.

When George passed away, I was overwhelmed with sadness, but not for me. I felt sadness for my boys who no longer had a father to share all of their amazing life experiences with. His death didn't hit me until the day after he passed away. It was just another day driving to the office in the early morning. A relaxing drive, no traffic, and the soothing sounds of my radio playing in the background. A song came on called "Two Occasions" by The Deele. Tears began welling up in my eyes as I listened to this song. This was the song George dedicated to me when we first met because making a cassette tape was one of the best ways to show your love in the '80s. Parts of our love were beautiful, but it wasn't enough to keep us together. I moved past the hurt and pain, and I was able to move on. I am thankful that we created two amazing, smart, handsome, and responsible boys. You left us too soon, George, and you will not get to see your grandkids grow up, but just know that they love you, Grandpa. You were and still are the best father the boys could have asked for.

Part Two

5

Unworthy of Love

"The only way to find true happiness is to risk being completely cut open."

- Chuck Palahniuk

The year is 2000. I was a single mother, free to do whatever I wanted to do. The feeling of freedom was amazing. I focused on my career, building the courage to divorce George when he was released from prison, and taking care of my boys. I was always very fortunate in my career and was able to get a job as a customer service representative at a car dealership. The position was a step down from the hotel, but it was going to pay the bills, so I took the job. My role was to contact the customers who came in for service to make sure everything was completed to their satisfaction. Part of this call was to ask them to take a survey. It was a very easy job, and some of my co-workers were nice people, but not all of them. Working at a car dealership, I was surrounded by mostly men. A lot of handsome, cocky, egotistical men—and somehow that attracted me. It was the same old bad-boy attraction!

I started to get close to one particular guy. He was handsome and charming with—guess what—blue eyes. Yes, I was a sucker for blue eyes. His name was Logan. He made me laugh and we got along great. He wasn't like the other salesman and had a friendly personality. We started dating, and eventually, the overnight stays started happening. We mostly met up at my place since his place was just a room and didn't really fit two people. I guess you can say we were getting pretty serious. Or so I thought.

One day, I woke up to a letter on the counter. It was from Logan. He told me that I deserved better and that he couldn't commit to me. I was devastated. Once again, I had allowed someone into my world and my heart. He had met my boys, and I was falling in love with him. Why did this keep happening to me? I started to think that something was wrong with me. What was I doing wrong to scare these guys away? Why couldn't he commit to me? I kept thinking it was because I had children and too much baggage, but somehow, I managed to once again pick up the pieces to my broken heart and move on with my life. I think at this point it was getting easier to move on since I was so used to it, but deep down, my heart was hurting.

I didn't want to work at the car dealership anymore because I knew that I would have to see Logan, so I decided to quit and look for another job. Thankfully, I landed another job pretty quickly at a start-up tech company. I had never worked for a start-up company, but I had heard from people in the industry that you could potentially get rich if you had stock options and the company went public. Who doesn't want to get rich quick? I accepted and signed the offer letter to join the company. I was hired as an administrative assistant, and the job was both easy and rewarding. The best part about working for this company was the people and the happy hours we all did together. There were two people with whom I started to form a special bond: a girl named Janet and a guy named Matt. Janet was a smart, attractive, fun, flirty, and lively girl. She was so full of life and I totally loved her energy. I felt smart when I was around her because she knew so much about computers and programming. Matt was a handsome, smart, attractive guy with the most beautiful piercing blue eyes—another blue-eyed guy who mesmerized me each time I talked to him! I don't know what it was with the blue eyes and why I kept being drawn to them.

Shortly after I started the job at the start-up company, I received word that George was going to be released from prison. When I heard the news, I was happy because I was finally going to be free from him permanently and the boys would get their father back. I couldn't wait to file for divorce and move on with my life, free of all commitments. I knew that I had to be strong and stay committed to what I wanted so that I wouldn't be lured back by his sweet talk. I decided to talk to some Buddhist members for advice, and they told me to chant for the strength and courage to divorce George. They also told me to chant for his happiness. According to The New Human Revolution, Vol. 19, "As we do our best for the welfare of others, we break out of our narrow lesser self, focused only on personal concerns, and gradually expand and elevate our life state. The commitment to others' well-being propels us to transform our own life condition and carry out our own human revolution." I took their advice and chanted every day for strength, courage, and happiness for myself and others.

My chanting paid off and the divorce proceedings went well with no issues or challenges. George still wasn't happy about the divorce, and he wasn't the nicest person to co-parent with, but I didn't care because he no longer controlled my life. Our divorce was finalized by the end of 2000. I was legally free to make my own decisions and do whatever I wanted.

I thought that I would be over-the-top happy that George and I were not married, but for some unknown reason, I still felt sadness inside. I had gotten everything I wanted, and I struggled to understand where this sadness could be coming from. Once again, I turned to my Buddhist practice and chanted daily for clarity and what was next in my life.

In our divorce agreement, George and I agreed to have joint custody of the boys. In the agreement, there would be no child support and we were both on our own financially to care for the boys. The boys continued to attend school near George's parents' house so that they could go there before and after school. The schedule for them was very unstable at the beginning of our divorce, and George didn't want to change to a schedule that was easier on the boys. He was still very angry at me for divorcing him, and he wanted me to feel it, so he used the boys a lot. I begged and pleaded with him to meet me halfway for the boys' sake, but it was going to be his way or the highway. After months of dealing with the chaotic schedule he made for us, we finally came to an agreement that worked for all of us.

With the new schedule, I had a lot of free time on my hands. I was still working at the start-up company and continued to form my bond with Janet. She knew all the hot spots to hang out at and was quite the party girl. When I was with Janet, I felt like I was free to do whatever I wanted to do. This was an amazing and exhilarating feeling. No responsibility, even if it was only temporary. I felt like I was making up for lost time not having my teen years and getting married so young. I was out of control and started drinking a lot. When I wasn't out with Janet at the clubs or bars, we were at work drinking off-hours with our co-workers.

But despite all the fun I was having, there was still something missing inside me but I couldn't figure it out. I was single and having fun—what more could a girl ask for? And yet, I still craved love and was so lonely. One night after drinking with co-workers, Matt offered to drive me home. Ah yes, the mesmerizing dreamy blue eye guy. I should have said no, but I was so attracted to him and craving so much love that I didn't resist. I wanted him to take me home. I wanted more than that from him. I forgot to tell you one important detail. Matt was married with children, and I knew his wife . . .

I knew that if he took me home, I would not be able to resist the temptation. Despite all my mixed feelings, I let it happen. Once we got to my place, I invited him in for a drink. I was so nervous. Was I really going to go through with this and have an affair with a married man? This was against everything that I believed in. I had been cheated on by my husband, and I knew that doing this was going to hurt people. Matt started to caress my hands as we sat near each other on the couch. My body was trembling with excitement as he pulled me closer to him. Our lips touched for the first time, and it felt like a bolt of lightning running through my body. He was an amazing kisser. As he started to remove my clothes, all the thoughts I had of him being married evaporated, and we had the most amazing, mind-blowing sex.

The affair with Matt went on for months. The sneaking around was a huge turn on for both of us, and it became an addiction. Late nights or even afternoons in the office, we would sneak into a conference room and have sex, or I would pleasure him orally. He loved it. The secret sneaking around made our sex even more exciting. Even though it was supposed to only be sex and nothing more, I started getting stronger feelings for Matt. I didn't want to be a home-wrecker, though my actions said something different.

I knew that the affair had to stop sooner rather than later, so I decided to not see him anymore. It was a quick and easy thing to do, but inside, I felt like a shitty person. And my inner critic voice would soon get worse. Shortly after Matt and I ended the affair, the company started to do layoffs, and I was on the chopping block. To me, this was a blessing in disguise. I didn't have to see Matt anymore and could move past this dark secret. I often wondered why a happily married man would go outside his marriage. Matt claimed that he loved his wife and kids but was having his fun with me on the side. The unavailable emotionally and physically men became the relationships I attracted in my life.

I always had good karma getting jobs, and I quickly landed another position that paid better. I had met a maintenance guy at the gym in the same business complex as the start-up, and he told me that his company was hiring an administrative assistant. I didn't know anything about property management, but it sounded like a good opportunity and I needed to build my career again. He told me that the job involved collecting rent for commercial buildings, paying property invoices, and supporting the property managers with whatever they needed. I interviewed and got the job.

I finally felt like my life was headed in the right direction, but I still felt this sense of unworthiness, loneliness, and sadness. I couldn't shake these feelings no matter how hard I tried. I had a better-paying job and I was able to support myself and the boys, but I still wanted to be in a relationship so badly. I craved for someone to love me. It was a craving that I thought would make me happy and take all my sadness away. I remember seeing couples out on the street or in restaurants, and instead of feeling happy, I felt jealous that I didn't have that. I felt like I was not good enough, and I worried that maybe I was going to be alone for the rest of my life. Then one day, I received a call from Logan. He missed me and wanted to see me. Because of the way I was feeling, I didn't even think twice before I agreed to see him. Was this a sign that I should be with him?

When I saw Logan again, I was still confused and upset about how he broke up with me, so I made up a story about how I was seeing someone. It wasn't true, of course, but I wanted him to feel the pain he put me through. He tried asking me questions about this new guy I was seeing, but I didn't give him any answers. He apologized for the way he broke up with me and admitted that it was a big mistake. He wanted to get back together. I was very hesitant because I didn't trust him. How could I trust him with my heart if he broke it the first time? I told him I needed time to think, and I agreed to see him again and just talk, nothing more. I was unsure if I was ready to let him back in my life. I didn't want to get back together out of desperation, but I'm not going to lie and say I didn't feel warm and fuzzy inside because a guy was actually pursuing me.

Our conversation was going really well—better than I expected. We were both in good spirits and I instantly remembered why I was so attracted to him in the first place. His warm smile took away all of the confusion I was feeling. Suddenly, in the middle of our conversation, he pulled out a small jewelry box and gave it to me. He said to me, "You are my girl, will you marry me?" Logan knew he'd made a mistake leaving me and didn't want me to be with anyone else but him.

I was in shock but at the same time full of joy. Someone wanted to marry me. He wanted to marry me even though I had an ex-husband and two small boys that he soon would be a stepfather to. Was I finally going to be in a loving, honest, and respectful relationship? I said "Yes."

I was ecstatic to plan the wedding. My wedding to George was not traditional, so I was determined that this wedding would have everything I ever wanted. I planned to have all of the things that come along with a traditional wedding: wedding party, cake, music, reception, bachelorette party, and a white wedding dress with a veil. Logan let me plan all the details exactly as I wanted them. I wanted a beach wedding, so we decided to have the ceremony on a cliff overlooking a beautiful beach. The reception would follow after at a hotel nearby on the ocean. I knew it was going to be a beautiful wedding, and I felt content. Pretty soon, all the sadness and loneliness began to dissipate. I knew that I wanted to be married to Logan for the rest of my life and we were going to live happily ever after. I couldn't have been happier.

Logan and I married in August 2001. It was a breezy and beautiful day. We were surrounded by all of our friends and family. My two boys, Junior and Romeo, were in the wedding party, and they looked adorable in their tuxedos. I had a spaghetti-strap white dress with beautiful pearl beading and small pink roses. My delicate white veil was attached underneath my bun hairstyle. As the limousine drove up to the venue, I started to feel the nerves setting in. I was getting married again, and all I could think about was: *What if Logan treats me like George did?* I didn't want to go through another heartbreak, and I couldn't bear to put my boys through another unloving environment.

But as soon as my feet hit the sand, and I saw Logan from a distance, all the nervousness went away. My dad walked me down the small sandy walkway to the edge of the cliff where we were to be married. Logan looked handsome in his tuxedo as he stood there to take my hand. It was very windy that day, and I remember my veil kept getting in the way of our ceremony. We managed to get through our vows even with all the wind and happily said "I do." I felt complete and whole in that moment. We had a wonderful photographer take our wedding pictures. The view was absolutely breathtaking, and we wanted to take advantage of the scenery so we took a short walk down to the beach below and captured beautiful shots by the ocean. It was truly a magical and perfect day.

Our reception was held at an incredible hotel ballroom overlooking the ocean. The waves were strong that day, and I remember them crashing against the rocks below. Our family and friends were all waiting for us as we walked into the ballroom as husband and wife. The party kicked off to the song "Celebration" by Kool and The Gang. Everyone was on the dance floor having a blast. Our DJ was entertaining and kept the night going smoothly with everyone having fun. We had games, a money dance, champagne toast, cake cutting, and garter and bouquet tosses. My new sister-in-law worked at a winery so we had top-of-the-line wine. The food was amazing, and the whole reception was everything I imagined and more.

The next day, we left for our week-long honeymoon at an all-inclusive resort in Jamaica. The resort we stayed at was heavenly, and we made beautiful love on this breathtaking island. We had an amazing time touring around, eating delicious food, and spending time on the beach. Logan was fair-skinned, and the first day he got a really bad sunburn that blistered on his head. I felt so bad for him.

He had to stay out of the sun for at least a few days while I soaked up the sun in all its glory. Despite his sunburn, he still enjoyed himself. We received a good amount of money as gifts from our reception, so we were able to shop. The shops were located in areas that were very poor, and I was surprised to see a lot of people begging for money on the streets. I didn't realize Jamaica had this much poverty. This was the only part of the trip that I didn't like. All good things had to come to an end, and it was time for us to pack up and head home. At this point in my life, I felt good about my relationship with Logan and happy about the future that he and I would be sharing. I still had a lot of insecurities that I carried from my first marriage, but I wanted to move past it all and not bring it into my marriage with Logan. I was determined to make this marriage work.

Self-Love Lesson:

"Document the moments you feel most in love with yourself- what you're wearing, who you're around, what you're doing. Recreate and repeat."

- Warsan Shire

6

Attack on America

"Go for it now. The future is promised to no one."

- Wayne Dyer

Logan and I could not afford to purchase a home, so we decided to rent and save money to hopefully buy a house in the future. We rented a cute one-bedroom apartment that was the perfect size for the two of us. Logan continued his job at the car dealership and I continued my job as an administrative assistant at the property management company. Then the impossible happened. The date was September 11, 2001. I was at work, and I heard my co-workers yelling in the breakroom. I went in to see what was happening. On the TV was a burning tower. I had no idea what was going on and asked one of my co-workers what was happening. She told me the Twin Towers at the World Trade Center in New York City were just hit by airplanes. I guess I was not educated enough, but didn't know what the Twin Towers were and someone had to explain it to me. I immediately contacted Logan to ask him if he was watching the news. I couldn't work for the rest of the day and requested to leave early so that I could be with my husband and children. This news was so devastating and heartbreaking. I didn't understand the severity of what was happening.

Over the next few hours, we kept getting more news updates. There weren't just two planes involved, and it wasn't an accident like everyone thought. The news was pouring in with reports on more attacks, and you could see people jumping out of the towers. I felt so sad and couldn't stop crying. Logan was doing his best to comfort me and to let me know that we were going to be OK. He wasn't going to let anything happen to me. I couldn't help but wonder what would have happened if we were still in Jamaica. We would have been stuck over there because all air travel was grounded. We were blessed to have come home just before all of this started.

As the weeks went by, more confirmed news came out about the attacks. This was a planned attack by nineteen militants associated with the Islamic extremist group al Qaeda. This group hijacked four airplanes and carried out suicide attacks against various targets in the United States. It was confirmed that two of the planes were flown into the World Trade Center in New York City, a third plane hit the Pentagon just outside Washington, D.C., and the fourth plane crashed in a field in Shanksville, Pennsylvania. The number of deaths rose as the weeks went by. The confirmed death toll was 2,996 people, even though there was speculation that the numbers were higher. I was overwhelmed with sadness for the families that lost loved ones. To them, it was just another day saying goodbye to each other, not knowing that they would never see each other again.

I started to reflect on my own life and loved ones. I became more appreciative of all the blessings that life had to offer me. I hugged and kissed my boys differently. I made it a point to say I love you every day to my boys and husband. I didn't want them to leave the house without them knowing how much they are loved. Life was definitely different after the 9/11 attacks. The world changed, and we now had to get used to a new normal. I was craving for any type of good news, and I wanted to get away from all the negativity that was going on in the world.

It was finally fall, and I always loved this season. In fact, fall was my favorite season of the year. I loved the smell of the first rains and how all the leaves changed colors. I was so wrapped up in my happy feelings of the fall season that I didn't realize what was happening to my body. I was due to have my period and missed it. I thought to myself, I can't be pregnant. Logan and I talked about having children but didn't want them so suddenly. I wanted to be married for at least a year and enjoy our time as a couple before having children. George and I had kids too early in our marriage, and I couldn't help but think this was part of the reason why things fell apart. Logan, however, wanted to have children of his own and didn't want to wait. I think that was his plan the entire time, and I was open to it because I knew it would make him happy. I finally agreed to get a pregnancy test and, to my surprise, I was pregnant. I was going to be a mother again. I didn't think I was a good mother to the two boys that I had. Probably from all the brainwashing George did to me when we were married. He always told me I was a horrible mother and I guess it stuck with me. How was I going to be a good mother to another child?

Logan was so excited, and I wanted to be a good wife, so I pretended to be just as excited as he was. But deep down, I was scared. I was afraid that I wouldn't be able to balance the needs of my marriage and my boys with new motherhood. All of the fears of failure from my first marriage started to surface. I couldn't help but think that having another child was going to interfere with my wonderful marriage with Logan. We were getting along so great, and I only had my boys half of the time so we had a lot of quality alone time. I was only in my first weeks of pregnancy and already had all of these unfortunate thoughts, but after a few weeks of worrying, I finally decided to just embrace it. I was always good at turning my thoughts around quickly. I figured if this was going to happen, I had better put on my happy face and enjoy the journey.

Since it had been six years since the birth of my last child, I didn't have any of the things you need for a baby. I had gotten rid of everything from my previous pregnancies, so I had a lot of fun shopping for new baby items. We also planned to have a baby shower, which helped cover a lot of the things we needed. I really started to feel happy, and I embraced the idea that it was going to be a wonderful experience.

I continued working full time until I was able to take maternity leave. I wanted to share my exciting news with my manager, so I went to work one day and asked to meet with her privately so that I could share the good news. We went into a conference room and sat down facing each other. I said to her, "I have some exciting news to share with you!"

She seemed excited as well and said, "Oh, what is it?"

I said, "I'm pregnant!"

Her face instantly turned to anger. I couldn't understand why my exciting, happy news would make her so angry.

She said, "Don't be surprised if the girls are not happy for you."

By this, she meant my female co-workers—but I didn't understand how she could be so unsupportive and cold.

When I asked her why they wouldn't be happy for me, she said, "Because you just started working here and now you will be taking maternity leave."

She was telling me the reason, but something didn't seem right. I knew there was more behind her insensitivity, but I let it go. I felt hurt inside, and my excitement and happiness turned to sadness. I wanted her support, but I didn't get any.

Then one day my manager came into work and announced that she was pregnant. Regardless of how she reacted to my news about being pregnant, I was happy and congratulated her. We were going to be pregnant together, and it felt like we had a connection in that sense. As the months went by, we were both getting bigger and bigger by the day. I had such an easy pregnancy—no issues with nausea or vomiting—but my manager didn't have the same experience. She couldn't hold anything down, not even water. I felt so bad for her.

After a few months, she started to treat me differently. She suddenly gave me a hard time about the tasks I completed and started being overly critical of my work. She would even give me the dirtiest look if I ate in front of her. I had to go somewhere else just to eat my lunch. I didn't like how she was treating me, but I knew I had to stay until after the baby was born to find another job.

Logan eventually left the car dealership and started another job where he was paid a regular salary instead of only commission. We wanted to save as much money as possible before the baby arrived. Everything was working out for the best, and we felt good about our decisions. Logan wanted to pick out the baby name, and he came up with David. I thought it was a cute name, so I agreed. I never asked where he got that name from—but I should have. I was eight months pregnant, and one night while we were at the movies watching *A Beautiful Mind*, Logan turned to me and asked, "Do you know how I got that name, David?"

I said to him, "No, how?"

"David was going to be the baby name that my first wife and I picked out."

My initial reaction was shock, and then it quickly turned to hurt. Why would he name our first son after a name that he and his ex-wife chose? I knew that he had been married before and that they'd never had children, but his decision left me feeling unimportant and confused. Our relationship was going well, and I'd let him back into my life again—even after he'd broken my heart. I trusted him to take care of me and my heart. I wanted to cry, but I held it back. I sat silently in the loud theatre while he turned away like it was nothing and continued to watch the movie. I should have spoken up and told him that I didn't want that name for our son. I should have told him that we should pick our own name. It was *our* first child—not his and his ex-wife's. I wanted the birth of our son to be a special time for both of us. But as usual, I held all of my feelings in and didn't say anything. I let my fears of speaking my truth remain unheard. This was the same behavioral pattern I had been living with since I was a child. Desperate to keep Logan happy, I sacrificed my feelings and happiness for him. David was going to be our first son's name, and there was nothing I could do or say to change it.

We went on with our life, and the baby name choosing conversation was a thing of the past. Little did I know, the silence was destroying my heart little by little each time. Our son David was born in May 2002. David's birth was serene compared to my two other boys. My water bag broke at home, and I had him six hours later. I had to get an episiotomy from a small tear while giving birth, but that was the extent of what my body went through. David was a beautiful baby boy. He was light-skinned, and he had brown hair with blonde tips. I had never seen hair like this on a baby! It was so unique and adorable.

I decided I was not going to breastfeed David. I had tried it twice before, but it always hurt like hell and I didn't like it. I had fears that the decision to not breastfeed would be like picking out the baby name and that it would be solely Logans decision. Amazingly, Logan supported my decision not to breastfeed. We stayed in the hospital for only a day before we were released to go home. I didn't have the same feelings of nervousness going home with David. I guess what I heard was true and that it does get easier the more kids you have—but was I a better mother? At least this time, I wasn't going to be a part-time mother to David. I was determined to be the best mother for all of my boys.

It had been six years since the birth of Romeo, and it was like we were starting all over again as new parents. The fear of failing as a mother kept creeping into my mind. The more I thought about failing as a mother, the more depressed I got. I hated myself for these thoughts, and I didn't know where all of this was coming from. I wasn't practicing my Buddhism at this time because Logan didn't support me, so I gave up practicing to focus on raising David and my marriage.

But months after giving birth to David, I started having strong feelings of self-doubt, sadness, confusion—and, according to Logan, severe mood swings. Why did I feel this way? I didn't want Logan to go through this with me. I was supposed to be happy with my new-born baby, not clogged with so many emotions that weren't serving me. Logan and I were also starting to argue a lot. We would fight about the little things like dirty dishes in the sink or clothes on the ground. I know that I was difficult to be around, so I decided to see my doctor to get some clarity on what was happening to me. After explaining my symptoms, the doctor told me that I had a medical condition called postpartum depression. Then it dawned on me and I suddenly remembered that I had this condition when I gave birth to Romeo. They gave me a pamphlet on the condition, and after reading it, I understood it more but was still in denial. How could I get this condition again? The doctor recommended a few treatment options, including mental health therapy or antidepressants. But I didn't want to do either. I was worried that I'd look like a crazy person, so I said "thank you" and left the doctor's office for home. I drove home in denial and kept telling myself that nothing was wrong with me. I swore I would get through it on my own.

The depression never really went away. Logan and I had only been married for a year and our marriage was already taking a turn for the worse. We didn't see things the same way, and our views on raising David were completely different. For instance, he decided that he didn't want to vaccinate David. I didn't agree with him and asked him what his reasoning was. He told me that he had done a lot of research on vaccinations and he didn't agree with what they were made of. He argued that natural immunity was better than immunity acquired through vaccinations. He also believed that if David got sick, he would overcome it better because his immune system would be stronger. I thought he was insane. I explained that both he and I had been vaccinated as children and we were fine, but he was adamant with his decision. Yes, it was *his* decision—it felt like we were back to choosing the baby's name. I had no say in the matter, so I was forced to remain silent. The doctors even thought he was crazy not to vaccinate, but Logan was set on his decision and my opinion or thoughts didn't matter. I had to go along with what he decided. I was back in that place when I was married to George and couldn't express how I felt or voice my opinion about the decision being made. I felt my body shaking with frustration. I was angry and upset. I was David's mother, and yet I wasn't allowed to have an opinion or decide what was best. In my head, I thought, *why didn't I know this before we got married?* We never discussed the timing on when we were going to have children let alone how we would raise them. Once again, I felt like I was in a marriage with no voice and nothing to say.

Self-Love Lesson:

"The most powerful relationship you will ever have is the relationship with yourself."

- Steve Maraboli

Comparing Lives

"Begin doing what you want to do now. We have only this moment, sparkling like a star in our hand, and melting like a snowflake."

- Marie Ray

I didn't want to focus on my marital problems with Logan, so I decided to concentrate on my career and furthering my education. This pattern felt so familiar—it was the same thing I did with George when we were having problems. I didn't want to be home with Logan. I wanted my freedom, even if it was just for a few hours. The issue was we didn't have the money for me to attend a traditional four-year college, and I also didn't have the time to attend school full-time since I was working and had children to care for. After doing some research online, I found a program that would accommodate my busy schedule. The program was through the University of Phoenix, and I only had to attend class one night per week in the evening. The location was close to my home and the program was accelerated so I would graduate quickly. I chose a program in business management that allowed me to focus on one class and subject at a time, each of which were five to six weeks long. I also qualified to get a student loan to pay for the classes.

My classes started immediately after I registered. In the beginning, it was very taxing working the entire day and going to school at night. I eventually got used to the long days, and I started to meet new friends. Part of the class requirements was to meet in a group and complete assignments together. I found a small group of people that became my study group, and before long, they became some of my closest friends. They were a lot of fun to hang out with, and we regularly connected outside of school. I became close friends with two of the girls in particular. I'm not sure if it was their energy or their beauty, but something about them just drew me in. They were both gorgeous women who had big personalities and knew how to have fun. One was married and the other was single. At first, hanging out with them was fun, but after a while, I started feeling insecure about myself. The single girl was very flirtatious and always had a cool story about the men she was having sex with. Her name was Destiny. I always thought how exciting her life must be. She didn't have kids, she wasn't married, and she was free to do whatever she wanted. I became obsessed with her life and I couldn't help but compare myself to her.

One night I was hanging out with Destiny, and a conversation came up about our bodies—mostly talking about our breasts. I was complaining to her about having small breasts and wished I had bigger ones. I went on to say that I felt like a boy and hated the way my shirts looked on me.

She said to me, "Why don't you just get breast implants?"

I had never known of anyone who had them. I only knew about them from the internet and movies. She proceeded to tell me that she had small breasts just like me before she got implants. Her breasts looked perfect, and I was determined to find out how I too could have perfect, large breasts. I thought if I had bigger breasts, men would be attracted to me and I could have a fun and exciting life like she did. I know I was married, but a girl can dream, right?

I went home and tried to convince Logan to help me pay for breast implants. I explained to him that I wanted to make my clothes fit better. Of course, I didn't tell him why I *really* wanted them. He didn't agree with me getting them, anyway, and he didn't support me in the decision. Regardless, I kept it in my mind that one day I would get those breast implants, with or without his support.

I was excelling in my professional life and I found another industry that would shape my future career—I just didn't know it at the time. I resigned from my position as an administrative assistant and found an opportunity as an assistant property manager. I really enjoyed the property management industry, and I made it a personal goal to become a property manager one day. I was still disappointed in myself for not staying in the hotel industry, and I saw this as my second chance to get back on track and have a career where I could grow professionally—but more importantly, I wanted a career that would help me provide for my family.

I ended up loving working in this role, and I felt very accomplished. I worked hard to finish my bachelor's degree, and I knew this would get me to the next level in my career. I received my bachelor's degree in the summer of 2003. It was truly a special day. The navy-blue cap and gown fit me perfectly, and I could feel my body light up like a surge of electricity when I walked across the big stage in front of hundreds of people to receive my degree. I never had a graduation ceremony when I completed high school because going into independent studies would only give you a diploma for graduating. I was proud and excited to finally walk the stage. The weather was perfect, and having my family there meant the world to me.

After receiving my degree, I focused on my career and was excited about my future. My career was promising, but my marriage was falling apart. Logan and I were arguing a lot more, and pretty soon our marital problems came into sharper focus. I was always tired, and if I had any kind of down time, I would dedicate it to sleep. I was so tired that our sex life became totally obsolete. I know that Logan had his own needs, but I wasn't able to fulfill them—nor did I want to. He would get really upset with me and tell me that I was always sleeping. Not only did he want more from me sexually, he also wanted me to take care of David more, but I just didn't have the energy or desire to do either. He resented me for this.

We also argued about our finances. He had a job that was paying commission only, and I was furious with him because I always felt like I had to bring in a steady income. I was also the one who carried the family on health insurance. This burden weighed me down and I felt like the entire world was resting on my shoulders. We were not happy, and neither of us could figure out how we had gotten to this place. I blamed myself for not being a good wife and mother, and I blamed him for not being understanding of my needs.

Despite our struggles, I still wanted our marriage to work—so one day, I mentioned to Logan that we should go see a marriage therapist. He agreed to go to couple's counseling, but it didn't help.

As we sat there in the therapy sessions, a common theme was him blaming me and me blaming him. Neither one of us wanted to admit fault to any of our issues in the marriage, so the sessions only pulled us farther apart. After a couple of sessions, he started to tell me that I was the crazy one and that I should go see a therapist on my own. I was quickly falling out of love with him, and I wanted out of the marriage. This felt all too familiar. Another failed marriage, and I was only thirty-one. The shame and disappointment I felt were weighing heavy on my heart. I loved being married, but I wanted my freedom at the same time. I was confused and lost. My heart was breaking and I didn't know how to mend it. Was I destined to be single for the rest of my life?

In January 2004, I decided to separate from Logan. I needed to be on my own to really know if staying in the marriage would be the best thing for both of us. I got a small one-bedroom apartment close by so that we could share taking care of David. Despite wanting to be on my own, I still wanted to be in a relationship. I still wanted to be loved even though my heart was broken. I thought if I could find someone else then I could divorce Logan and have the perfect loving relationship that I always wanted. I know what you are thinking—hasn't this girl learned her lesson yet? Well, I hadn't! And I have a lot more to share with you before we get there, but we will.

I started going through my mental Rolodex in the hopes of finding someone I could connect with, but I knew that I didn't want to contact anyone with whom I'd had a relationship before. Then it hit me. I remembered this guy that I worked with at the car dealership—and who I was extremely attracted to. His name was John. He had all of the exterior qualities I liked in a man. Yes, therein lies the problem. I was always attracted to the exterior before I got to know the interior. He was charming and tall, with nice hair, a warm smile, and beautiful green eyes. Yes, the eyes again. The piercing-colored eyes always drew me in. His personality was very mysterious. I could never figure out what he was thinking, and our conversations always left me wondering. This mysteriousness attracted me to him even more. I was always a curious girl, and solving a mystery was a huge turn on for me. I never pursued him in the past because I was dating Logan, but I always thought he was attractive.

I was able to track down his number and contacted him. I was trembling with excitement as he answered. His voice was deep and strong, just like I remembered it. As we started talking, he asked me why I was contacting him now. It had been a while, and he knew that I was married. I said to him, "I am separated right now and trying to figure things out."

We talked for hours, catching up on life and getting to know each other more. He told me that he was dating but I didn't care. I was caught up in the moment we were having and enjoying our conversation. Before we hung up, we agreed to keep in touch. We even set up a time to have dinner. As we said goodbye, all I could think of was kissing his lips.

As months went by, I was excelling in my career and I felt like my life was heading in the right direction. Separating from Logan seemed like it was doing wonders for our relationship. He and I were getting along great. It's funny how removing yourself from a tough situation can open your eyes to things you never saw or felt before. I was having fun with John and growing closer to him. He made me feel sexy and alive again, but I could only see him when he wasn't with his girlfriend. Sometimes I would be with him while he was talking to her on the phone. I remember the feeling of power over her. Here I was with her boyfriend, and she didn't have a clue. One night while she was out of town, John asked me to come over and spend the night with him. I didn't even have to stop and think about it—I said yes immediately.

When I arrived at his house, my morals started to mess with my mind. My body knew what it wanted, but my mind thought otherwise. As soon as I saw John, my body quickly took over and shut down my mind. He told me that he needed a few minutes to call his girlfriend to say goodnight. As he lay on his bed dialing her number, I couldn't help myself and walked over to where he was. I lay next to him as he was talking to her on the phone. I was turned on at how sexy he looked, and I slowly started to caress him on top of his pants. I could see how turned on he was, and that made me keep doing it. Then I slowly started to make my way down between his legs. He continued to talk to his girlfriend as I looked at him. I started to unzip his pants and gently pull out his penis. His body was quivering with excitement, but he couldn't say a word other than the words he was telling his girlfriend. I started to kiss and lick his penis up and down as his eyes rolled back into his head with extreme pleasure. He couldn't contain his excitement anymore and exploded with pleasure. I smiled at him as he said goodnight to his girlfriend.

John and I never had physical sex, and this oral pleasure became the thing that he wanted from me. This was the first time that I felt the power of revenge take over my soul—the very same revenge that I wanted from my first marriage to George. I wanted the other woman to feel the pain that I felt in my heart when my husband was cheating on me. If she found out about us, would she be heartbroken? Would she feel the same pain I did? In this moment, I knew that it was not only my heart that was broken—it was also my soul.

October was approaching, and Halloween was always a precious time well spent with the children. Driving the kids to the Halloween store to pick out their costumes always made me happy. The sounds of giggling and amazement in their eyes as we walked through the aisles made me think of my childhood. I didn't remember Halloween with my parents, and I vowed to make Halloween a time filled with enjoyment for my children.

This particular year, Logan and I were trying to figure out who would take David trick-or-treating, and we decided that it was too difficult to choose since we both wanted to do it. I missed our family time together, and I knew David would be happy if both of us took him. Halloween arrived, and it was the best time Logan and I had in a very long time. I had forgotten how much fun we used to have before we got married and had a child. We laughed and talked through the night. Our connection felt amazing, and my heart pumped with joy. I didn't go back to my place that night and stayed with Logan and David. As we all got ready for the night, David didn't want to sleep in his own bed. I knew that his excitement was from seeing me and Logan back together. We all jumped into bed as David lay between us, and he wore a smile that warmed my heart. As soon as he fell asleep, we moved him to his bed. It was a day to remember, and I wasn't going to let go of that feeling. My family was back together, and in this moment, nothing else mattered.

The following month, I noticed that I missed my period. I was thinking to myself, could I be pregnant again? Logan and I had what most people call make-up sex, but could it be true? I couldn't help but continue to beat myself up over the idea of having another baby and giving up my new freedom. But was I free? I was still married to Logan and had a child with him. Heck, I had two other boys that I was responsible for. I wasn't free from anything.

That night, I sat on my couch, miserable and out of my mind with the painful thoughts of giving up my freedom. Little did I know that the freedom I needed was not the physical part of being free, but the freedom I needed inside my broken heart. I needed to free my heart from all the pain in my past to move on. This would eventually come but not until years later. I knew what I needed to do. I needed to go back to Logan and try to make the marriage work. Especially if I was going to have another baby. Freedom was a word that didn't exist in my life and I needed to be the responsible mother and wife.

So once again, I picked myself up and made a doctor's appointment to take a pregnancy test. Sure enough, I was pregnant. The doctor came into the room with a great big "congratulations!" But that word felt like falling down a cliff without a rope and not being able to climb back up. I wanted to run and scream from the top of my lungs. How could I be that stupid? The hurtful inner voice was telling me that I was pathetic and weak. *You will go back to Logan and be the sad, sorry girl that you are. You were not happy with him and having another child with him will not make your marriage better.* I hated my inner voice, but I believed everything she said to me. As I got dressed and headed down the stairs to my car, the responsible wife and mother took over. I called Logan to give him the news. I could hear the excitement in his voice as I told him that we were having another baby. His excitement was contagious and made all of my doubts melt away like the fresh snow under the warm sun. The following month, I moved back in with Logan and stopped seeing John.

Moving back in with Logan was not as bad as I thought it would be. It was as if we were back when we first met. His charm and humor were shining through so brightly that I could feel my heart exploding with joy all over again. We were both filled with joy as we prepared for our second child's arrival into the world. Thankfully we had kept the baby items from when David was born. Money was tight, and we needed to save where we could. We started talking about baby names, and I was scared that he would choose the name as he did with David. As we were talking about choosing a baby name one day, I asked him if I could choose the name this time. We both liked the San Francisco Giants, and I was obsessed with JT Snow. JT Snow was a first baseman on the team, and I was his biggest fan. I said to Logan, "I want to name our baby after JT Snow." Surprisingly he didn't blink an eye, and he agreed. Finally, after carrying three babies and not being able to choose a baby name, I would name my fourth and final child. I definitely wasn't going to have any more children, and in this moment, everything felt perfect.

At this time in my life, I was still doing well in my career and still working as an assistant property manager towards my goal of becoming a property manager one day. Logan was still working commission jobs, which put a huge financial strain on our relationship. Our arguing picked back up again, and it was consistently about our lack of money. I still felt like I had to take care of the family financially and always had to cover the health insurance for everyone. Logan disagreed when I would tell him that I felt like I was the man in the relationship by carrying all the burden. It angered him that I felt this way. I know that it was hurtful to belittle his manhood, but I was upset at him for not providing more for the family. He was the man in the relationship, had a job, and was taking care of the family. He would tell me that he brought in more money than I did with the commission that he was making. My anxiety would build up every month because another argument would surface. I know that couples argue, but I was so tired of bickering with Logan about our finances. Did you know that money is the number one cause of disagreements between married couples?

JT was born in July 2005. His birth was easy compared to my other birthing experiences with my previous boys. The only complication I had (which really wasn't a complication) was a ton of pain in my left leg. The varicose veins looked like large tree roots going down from my thigh to my foot. The pain was so excruciating I had to wear a compression panty hose to help relieve some of the pressure. The doctors told me it was a common thing in many pregnant women, and that it would go away once the baby was born. I prayed for the pain and veins to go away. I was only in my 30s and I wanted to keep my legs looking nice. My legs were the only feature on my body that I had always loved.

I was only in labor for a short while, and I slept some of the time after I received the epidural. I was not going to be a superhero mom and go without that wonderful drug to relieve the labor pains. It was finally time to push and get this baby out into the world. I remember being so sleepy that even the bright lights shining above me didn't wake me up. I couldn't feel a thing from the waist down. In fact, I was so numb that I didn't even feel myself pushing. My doctor was a woman, and all I could remember is her telling me in her soft, tender voice to push. With every push, she would tell me that I was doing great. How could I be doing great if I didn't feel anything? I must have pushed three times with absolutely no feeling before JT came out. His first cries were the most beautiful sound, and just like my other birth experiences, my heart was filled with joy. The experience always felt new and like I was having a child for the first time. Tears of joy streamed down my face as I held my baby for the first time.

Self-Love Lesson:

"It's all about falling in love with yourself and sharing the love with someone who appreciates you, rather than looking for love to compensate for a self-love deficit."

- Eartha Kitt

8

Already Gone

*"Courage starts with showing up and
letting ourselves be seen."*

- Brene Brown

In the summer of 2007, Logan and I were at our all-time low in our relationship. We stopped communicating with each other, our intimacy died, we drifted apart, and we were arguing non-stop. At this point in my life, I was working in San Francisco and commuting on the Caltrain. Logan hated me working at this job because it kept me away from home all the time. I would leave for work when it was dark and return home when it was dark. The job placed a huge strain on our already damaged relationship, but I was determined to keep my career. I had already given up my dream of becoming a general manager of a hotel, and I'd be damned if I was going to give up this career too. I enjoyed working in San Francisco, and I felt like a different girl in a new city every day I went to work. Commuting by train took off a little of the stress from my day since I didn't have to drive. Some days I would continue working on the train, and the ride was always entertaining. There were always the regular commuters on the train, and I soon became close friends with a few of them. We sat together on the train, shared stories, and laughed the entire time.

There was one particular guy who got on the train at the same stop I did. His name was Hardy. He had a dry, egotistical personality, but I was extremely attracted to him. Why was I always drawn to this type of man? It wasn't what I wanted in my life, but I kept attracting it. I asked myself this question over and over again, but no answer ever came. It shouldn't come as a surprise that Hardy had the most amazing piercing blue eyes that stared right through my soul. I know . . . the eyes again! But Hardy's eyes were not like the rest—they reminded me of wolf eyes. He also had this macho energy about him that drew me in like a bad habit.

We started to sit next to each other on the train instead of with our train friends, even though I had a feeling that sitting next to him was going to put me in a situation that was not going to be good for either of us. He was engaged, and I was married—but I let my emotions take over like I always did and let him into my life. I wanted to bury the marital problems that Logan and I were having. This guy would be a beautiful distraction, and he didn't mind that I was married, which made the situation even easier. Each day that we sat next to each other on the train, the stronger my feelings grew. I never really knew how he was feeling because he was a very private guy. Our conversations were brief and mostly centered on work and children. I always got excited when he shared something personal about his life. One time I got a glimpse into his world when he told me he was a recovering alcoholic and didn't drink. Yes, I held onto this as his way of opening up to me—but in reality, he was basically telling me he was an addict and I was his new addiction.

Every day I looked forward to the train ride home because I knew that I would see Hardy. Then, one day, we took our relationship to the next level. Well, I felt like it was the next step, but really it was me massaging his hands with lotion. I know it sounds strange, but it was sexually arousing. I was so attracted to Hardy that I would do anything he asked me to do just to get closer to him. This massaging started to become a regular thing when he sat next to me. It was so robotic. He would sit down, place his hand in my lap, and hand me the lotion with no conversation. I guess I was a good hand massager because he always fell asleep. Hardy knew that I was sexually attracted to him because I was vocal about it one day. He alluded that he was sexually attracted to me too, but never told me in a direct way. He definitely knew how to pull my heart strings, and I let him.

I had my secret on the train and my career life in the city. I worked for a well-known property management company. The properties that I managed were all Class-A buildings located in the Financial District of San Francisco. My co-workers were all friendly, and the perks that I received were amazing. We would eat at fancy restaurants and sometimes after work we would go out to swanky bars for a cocktail. Then, one day, I couldn't get out of bed. Every time I moved, the room started to spin. My head felt like it was in a washing machine spinning on high speed. I couldn't get up to use the restroom because I would fall down. I made an appointment with the doctor, and after multiple tests, I was diagnosed with vertigo. According to an internet search, vertigo is a common problem with the way balance works in the inner ear, although it can also be caused by problems in certain parts of the brain. Vertigo can also be something called benign paroxysmal positional vertigo (BPPV), where certain head movements can trigger these feelings of dizziness and spinning. I thought to myself, *How could I get this? No one in my family has this.* The vertigo went away after a week of being bedridden, but my health problems got worse.

Then the vertigo came back, and I had a second episode that put me on bed rest once again. I started to lose a lot of weight and went from a size 6 to a size 0 in less than a year. I was losing so much weight that my clothes started to fall off of me. The doctors ran more tests, but everything came back fine. They finally came up with a diagnosis that it must just be stress. This diagnosis made perfect sense to me. Logan and I were constantly arguing about everything, especially about my work. I was drinking more than I normally did and not eating well. My stress level at work was high because I always had to rush to catch the train and get home before Logan got upset. This stress was putting a huge strain on my body.

One night, I arrived home from work and Logan gave me an ultimatum. He said to me, "You need to quit your job. It's either us or the job." This was my chance to leave, but I didn't want to break up our family, so I decided to start looking for another position closer to home. I was filled with anger that once again I was going to give up a career that I worked hard to get to. I wasn't going to see my train friends anymore, but most of all, I would never see Hardy again.

I started to apply to various positions and tried to stay within the property management industry, but I wasn't seeing any of these positions posted. I came across one job posting for a facility management position, and I felt like my skillset matched the job description, so I applied. A few weeks later, a hiring manager reached out to me about becoming a site facility manager. I guess since I had experience in property management, the skill set was transferable into facility management, which was an industry I had never heard of. At first, I thought to myself, *Do I have to clean toilets? What the heck is a site facility manager?* For those of you who don't know, basically, facility management (FM) is a profession that encompasses multiple disciplines to ensure functionality, comfort, safety, and efficiency of the built environment by integrating people, place, process, and technology. Despite my doubts, I decided to go in for an interview and was offered the job. I knew that this position would bring me closer to home and I would no longer have to commute to San Francisco. I wanted to save our marriage and make Logan happy.

Despite getting a new job closer to home (and satisfying Logan's demands), I couldn't help but wonder why I didn't just stay separated from him. I would have been happier on my own. But instead, I felt weak and like a failure. I had fallen so far out of love for Logan that I couldn't find my way back to that place in my heart where I could give him what he needed. The night I knew it was finally over was when Logan wanted to have sex. It wasn't anything new that he wanted from me, it was just different this night. I no longer wanted to give my body to him—I didn't love him and had so much resentment towards him for all the disagreements we had that never resolved. Most nights Logan would just let it go, but on this night, he was adamant that he get what he wanted. As we lay in the bed, I could feel the cold control in his voice touch my body as he said to me, "You are my wife and will give me sex." I felt like there was no other way out of this controlling situation, and I agreed to give my body to him. After we were done, he fell asleep. Tears of emptiness fell down my face, and my body was numb from the pain in my heart. I don't know how it feels to be raped, but on this night, I felt like I was. In this very moment, I knew that there was nothing more to give. It was over between Logan and me.

David was five and JT was two. Junior was eighteen and living with his dad most of the time, and Romeo was twelve and stayed with us every other weekend and some weekdays. I had the most amazing children, and I was blessed to be their mother, but I couldn't figure out why I felt like I didn't deserve them. I often had thoughts that I could just disappear and they would be better off without me. I was thirty-five and had already gone through one divorce, with another one on the way. I'd given birth to four children and managed to successfully hold down a steady career. How could someone at my age experience so much and yet feel like there was more to explore? I wanted to disappear from the life I had and start a new one. I even dreamed of changing my name so that no one would find me. I had no energy and was always tired. The voice of my inner critic was always in my head telling me that I was a failure and a weak, confused, stupid, horrible mother.

Logan and I separated in the winter of 2007. I remember the day I told him that I wanted a divorce. I thought it was going to be the happiest day of my life, but it wasn't. My heart was aching with every beat and breath that I took. I wanted to die. We both agreed that the best thing for the boys was for them to go with him, and I would get them every other weekend. At the time, I thought this was the best thing for my boys, but why did I feel so empty inside? I kept saying to myself that this is what I wanted, and I would finally be free from all responsibility in my life. But I still felt empty, and I started to second-guess my decision to divorce Logan—but it was too late. Logan and the boys moved out in December and moved to another town near his family two hours away. I felt a sense of peace knowing that they would be close to his family, but that didn't help the pain in my heart. My boys and husband were gone. I sat alone, silently crying, wishing for my happy marriage back and hearing our wedding song in my head, Shania Twain's, "You're Still the One." We didn't make it, and all bets that we were never going to make it won. Why couldn't we hold onto each other? Why couldn't we fight to save our marriage and family? We came so far but lost it all. I wasn't going to kiss him goodnight, and he wasn't the one anymore.

Self- Love Lesson:

"Don't sacrifice yourself too much, because if you sacrifice too much there's nothing else you can give and nobody will care for you."

- Karl Lagerfeld

As I reflect back on this part of my life, there are a lot of things that I would have done differently. But if I did things differently, the story would be over, and I have so much more to share with you. I had a blessed life with four wonderful boys and an amazing career. I just couldn't see past my insecurities and confusion. My journey wasn't over, and I would only realize years later that these experiences during this part of my life were lessons I needed to learn. I heard someone tell me one day, "Life is like school. It will serve you an exam over and over until you pass." I wasn't passing the exams, and I was still the broken person that was married to George. I carried a lot of my emotional trauma and baggage into my relationship with Logan. Both Logan and I deserved a healthy, loving, honest, and respectful relationship. I thought that I could give this to him, but I couldn't get past the turmoil in my head. Therapy was the right thing to do, and I know it now, but back then I was so uneducated that I thought therapy was only for crazy people. I didn't want to be classified as crazy, even though sometimes I felt like I was going crazy in my mind. I craved for love outside of myself, and I attracted people in my life based on my low self-esteem. I hated myself, and I didn't understand why—nor did I want to figure it out. I avoided confronting my fears, and I thought that if I just kept moving forward, things would get better. They didn't—and they only got worse. I allowed myself to go to an even darker place by doing things that I thought would make me happy. In the end, the happiness I was searching for just wasn't there, and it would push me further down the wrong path.

Part Three

9

On My Own

"I read and walked for miles at night along the beach, writing bad blank verse and searching endlessly for someone wonderful who would step out of the darkness and change my life. It never crossed my mind that that person could be me."

- Anna Quindlen

Remember the breast augmentation that I wanted? Guess what? I decided to go for it. I was finally in a place of freedom and able to make a decision without anyone controlling me. This was my chance to become the beautiful, sexy woman I longed to be. I thought men were going to love and want me more with my new large breasts. I met with a plastic surgeon my friend had recommended and immediately selected her to perform the surgery. I didn't want to shop around, and she checked off all the boxes that I was looking for in a plastic surgeon. She was female, she had performed many surgeries previously, and she was very educated in her field.

When I arrived at her office for a consultation, I was given a stack of paperwork to fill in before I saw the surgeon. As I walked down the hallway to the patient room, I felt very comfortable and calm. The assistant handed me a gown and asked me to undress from the waist up. The chill in the room made my nipples hard, and I started to feel embarrassed about it—but why did I feel this way? The doctor was a plastic surgeon, and she had seen hundreds of hard nipples.

Then there was a knock on the door, and it was the doctor. She introduced herself and proceeded to talk about my medical history and the paperwork I had just filled in. Then she showed me an album of before and after pictures. She asked me if I wanted saline or silicone and explained the differences between the two options. She explained how she would be placing the implants and that it would be both over and under the muscle. This would create a tear-drop effect and make it appear more natural. She asked me where I wanted the incision site. I could choose between a high crease in the underarm, at the inframammary fold underneath the breast, or around the lower border of the areola. She also asked what size implants I wanted. I didn't even know I had a choice! As she explained the options and procedure to me, I thought to myself, *Wow! All this just to get breast implants. So many choices and decisions to make.* I realized how uneducated and naive I was on the surgery and implants. Then it dawned on me: I had never had surgery before, and someone would be cutting into my body, opening me up, and implanting a foreign object into it. I suddenly felt my heart pounding and the palms of my hands were wet with sweat. What was I doing here? Why wasn't I happy with what I was born with? All I knew was that I hated my body, and I felt like getting these implants was going to make me happier and feel more like a woman. I qualified for a payment plan and scheduled my surgery.

My surgery was scheduled for December, and I considered this to be a Christmas gift to myself—the best Christmas gift anyone could ask for, right? What more could a girl with a broken heart who hated her body and who'd just lost her family want? I needed a ride home after the surgery since I was going to be heavily sedated and not allowed to drive, so I mustered up the courage to ask the ex-husband who I had just divorced. I remember asking Logan to pick me up, and his response was pretty comical. He said to me, "You want me to do *what*?" I told him that I didn't have anyone else to help me, and as he agreed to help me, I could hear the sarcasm in his voice, "How is this *my* problem?"

The big day finally arrived. I was nervously anticipating how I would look after surgery and excited that I would finally not have a boy body anymore. I would finally have a body I could be proud of.

Logan arrived to pick me up and take me to the surgery. The car ride was a long, awkward silence as we headed to the clinic. Logan even cracked a joke about the surgery and said to me, "Man, I'm not even going to be able to enjoy them." We finally arrived at the clinic. The check-in process was fairly smooth, then I was escorted to a room where I would wait until my surgery time. As I lay in the hospital bed—alone, nervous, and disoriented—all I could think was, *Am I really going to do this?* I was quickly interrupted when the nurse came in to let me know it was time. This was my last chance to back out. Thoughts were racing through my head at 60 mph. My heart was beating so fast, it felt like it was going to beat right out of my chest. As I was wheeled into the surgery room, I was transferred to another bed that was the perfect size for my body. It was almost as if they made the bed specifically for me. The last thing I remember was the anesthesiologist asking me to count backward from five.

Then there was the feeling of soft slapping on my cheeks. It was the nurse in her soft, sweet voice saying to me, "Wake up, sweetie." . . . Groggy and lifeless, I started to open my eyes. More slapping on my cheeks. "Wake up. You have boobs now." I still couldn't open my eyes as I felt a tight band wrapped around my chest. I felt like a baby elephant was sitting on me. After moments of disarray, I felt myself coming out of a magical dream. Logan was there to take me home, and I cannot recall how I got there. All I could remember is Logan dropping me off with my medication and saying goodbye. I slept for hours, but it felt like decades. When I finally woke up, the pain started to settle in. The pain was so excruciating that I wanted to go back to the doctor and tell them to remove the implants. I couldn't lift my arms, wipe my butt, or comb my hair. Simple life tasks were all of a sudden so difficult and I had no one to help take care of me.

Here I was, supposed to be super happy, but I still felt an overwhelming sadness inside of me. I thought this familiar feeling was going to vanish once I got the breast implants. I thought that if I could get rid of the pain, then maybe this would take my sadness away. I was given a pain killer called Percocet, which is something I had never taken in my life. I took it for a few days before I started noticing that my face looked like death took over. I was depressed and taking painkillers. Sounds like a bad cocktail, right? I decided to stop taking the Percocet and stuck to something I was more familiar with: extra-strength Tylenol.

I was slowly starting to feel like myself, but I still couldn't sleep lying down. My back was a mess from being hunched over because I wasn't used to all this extra weight on my chest. I contacted my girlfriend Melinda, whom I met on the train when I used to commute to San Francisco. I hadn't talked to her in a while and I really needed some cheering up. She was always so bubbly and righteous in her own way. I loved her positive energy and personality. I knew talking to her would make me feel better. She was just as excited to hear from me. I started explaining to her how depressed I was feeling and that I still couldn't sleep properly which was causing me to be so exhausted. She accepted me with open arms and asked me to come over and spend the night. It was truly the happiest feeling knowing that someone actually cared and was going to take care of me. This was the beginning of our beautiful spiritual friendship and my long journey towards loving myself. My friend Melinda taught me how to look at the positive side of things and affirm every day that I am worthy and deserving of love. She showed me what it was like to be righteous in my own way and encouraged me to be confident in myself. Her ability to move from a negative place to a positive place gave me hope for a happier life.

The month of December came and went, and in the blink of an eye, it was January 2008. I was settling into my new single life, and Melinda and I were growing closer and closer with our friendship. She started teaching me how to love myself and showed me what worked for her. She taught me more about affirmations and told me to write down on a Post-It note what kind of person I wanted to be and place it where I could read it every day. So I wrote down a few things: *I am worthy of love. I am loved. I am confident.* I hung the notes on my bathroom mirror because I knew that would be a place I would go every day. I also knew that looking at myself in the mirror and saying positive things out loud to myself would have more of an impact on how I felt. At first, I called bullshit on her advice. I thought to myself, *I do love myself. Why would I not love myself?* I was perfect now with my new breasts and my new freedom. Right?

But the truth is, my new breasts and freedom did not make me happy. I was sinking fast into negativity, and I needed help. Melinda stressed the importance of continuing to write down what I wanted in life and read them every day. She taught me about the power of the universe and how I can transform my negative thoughts into positive ones by affirming what I want in life. I continued writing down my goals, and I made a vision board with all of the things I want in life. Even though I was still in disbelief, I decided to try what she was teaching me—at this point in my life, I would do anything to find happiness. So I started affirming and writing down in a journal what I wanted in life. I brought positivity into my home, car, and work. I consistently put positive thoughts into my head whenever I started to think a negative thought. I read positive quotes every day, and I even started posting on my social media because I felt that if I put good vibes out to the Universe, positive things would come back to me.

I started to feel better about myself, and I loved affirmations so much that I became obsessed with them. I wanted to know everything and anything about positive affirmations, and I started to research everyone who taught about positivity. One night on the internet, I came across a writer named Louise Hay. I found her webpage and read through her healing techniques and positive philosophy. Her writings told me that I could create more of what I wanted in my life, body, mind, and spirit. This sounded amazing—I wanted a life full of my desires and dreams, but most of all, I wanted to be happy. I still had my doubts about how affirmations could change my life, but I felt like it was doing something because I was starting to feel better each day after reading them. I decided to purchase my first deck of affirmation cards called "Power Thought Cards." This was the first deck of affirmation cards that I invested in. I didn't know it then, but this was the best investment of my life. Every day I anticipated the arrival of my deck of cards.

They finally arrived, and opening the box was like Christmas time for my soul. Have you ever received a gift that was good for your soul? The description on the deck of cards read: "This deck of 64 affirmation cards will help find your inner strength. Each vibrant card contains a powerful affirmation on one side and a visualization on the other to enlighten, inspire, and bring joy to your life." Sounds amazing, right? Who doesn't want to enlighten, inspire, and bring joy to their lives? This was something I had wanted since I was sixteen years old. Now, here I was, thirty-six years old, and I still hadn't found my true happiness and joy.

I pulled my first random card from the deck, and on the front, it read, "I trust the process of life." The back read, "There is rhythm and flow to life, and I am part of it. Life supports me and brings me only good and positive experiences. I trust the process of life to bring me my highest good." Reading this card resonated with me, so I hung it on my bathroom mirror and read it every morning.

As the weeks went by, I started to feel better about myself. I began to visualize my life changing. My life seemed to get better, yet I still couldn't get past my fear of being alone. Deep down, I still felt like I needed a man in my life to be happy. As I sat on my couch contemplating who would be the next man in my life, the phone rang. It was George's sister. Yes, apparently if you have children with a man, they never actually leave your life—but everything was about to change. I could hear the panic in her voice as she told me that George was just picked up by the U.S. Immigration and Customs Enforcement (ICE). I sat quietly in disbelief on the phone as she explained what happened. (For those of you who don't know, ICE is the federal agency in charge of stopping cross-border crime and illegal immigration.) As she was saying this, I couldn't understand why they would want to pick up George—and then I remembered that he wasn't a U.S. citizen. He had a green card, which was a permit allowing a foreign national to live and work permanently in the U.S. George would always tell me that he didn't want to become a U.S. citizen because if we went to war, he didn't want to be the first person to be thrown out of the plane. I know, what the heck?! Who in their right mind would think this? Well, George wasn't always in his right mind.

We found out later that George was hiding from ICE, and when he was released from prison, he was supposed to be deported. You see, when you commit a felony in the U.S., you are supposed to be deported if you are not a citizen. George never mentioned this to me or his family. We were all in shock. ICE was conducting a series of raids in California, and George happened to be part of their five-year push targeting immigrants who ignored their deportation orders or returned to the United States illegally after being deported. George was deported and not allowed to return to the United States. My heart sank for my boys. I knew what it was like to grow up without a father, and I never wanted this for my children. Junior was nineteen and Romeo was thirteen at the time, and once again, they would have to grow up with no father in their life.

Here I was, a single mother at the age of thirty-six with no child support and no partner in my life. Junior was off to college and Romeo went to go live with my mother while I got my life together. I know, why would I send my child to someone who never showed me love? The strange thing is my mother wasn't the way she was with me as a child. She loved her grandkids and she would do anything for them. It was like she was a completely different person with the boys. She was loving, nurturing, and caring, but she still had the strictness. I don't think that was ever going to go away. It was only supposed to be a temporary living situation, but it ended up being five years. The guilt I carry still haunts me today, but I know that I couldn't have given my kids what they needed at the time, which was my love. My heart was broken into pieces and my soul was lost. My depression was worsening by the day, and I couldn't figure out why I was so unhappy. I was crying on a daily basis and searching endlessly for my true happiness. I was still reading positive affirmations every day, but it wasn't enough to get me through the day. Going to sleep was the best part of my day because I knew that was the time when I didn't have to think about my unhappy life. I started practicing Buddhism again, and I chanted with conviction to be happy. I was willing to try anything and everything to find happiness and love.

A friend of mine mentioned to me that I should see a therapist. She said that maybe talking to someone neutral would help resolve some of my unwanted feelings. I knew that seeing a therapist would help me, but I was still resistant to it. I kept telling myself that I could get through my struggles on my own and didn't need a therapist. What could a stranger tell me to make me feel better if they knew nothing about me? Instead of sulking in my unloving misery, I decided to focus on what I knew best: my career. At this point, I was doing well in my role but still not satisfied with the responsibilities I was given. The job didn't require me to use my brain, and I felt like there was more to learn in the facility management industry. I started to feel bored when I went to work. Of course, what do you do when you are bored? I started to look for distractions, and I found one at work.

I met my distraction in the fall of 2008. His name was Paul, and we worked together in the same department. Paul was charming, handsome, unbelievably smart, and he had the most amazing brown eyes. Surprise, no blue eyes! What a nice change for me. I think I was more attracted to his brains than anything. Paul was six years younger than me, so I wasn't sure it would work out. He was exactly what I didn't need after a second failed marriage and suffering from severe depression, but I ignored my inner critic and decided to give him my number. At first, we were just friends and went to lunch together. Things were different with Paul. He was respectful of my feelings and truly wanted to get to know me. We became very close, and I shared a lot of my life experiences with him. Paul hadn't had a lot of previous relationships, so my life to him was always more interesting. He knew I had children and had been married previously, but he didn't seem to have a problem with it at the time. I was open with him about my separation from Logan, but that got no reaction from him. I was still a married woman. How could this not bother him? It was a question I should have dug deeper for an answer, but I was just smitten from meeting a nice guy.

Our relationship was progressing so fast that I felt like I was in the Daytona 500 racing for the prize. Soon after our work lunch dates, we started spending time outside of work and it started to get serious. We decided to keep our relationship private—mostly because I was still a married woman and we didn't want anyone at work to know we were in a relationship. We talked on the phone for hours and sent morning texts to each other. We were crazy about each other, and neither of us could contain the strong emotions that were overcoming us. I remember the first time we kissed. My lips against his was like warm honey butter on cornbread. It had been a while since I had kissed someone so passionately, and I'd forgotten what it felt like until I kissed Paul. He reminded me of how a steamy, passionate kiss can light up your entire body with electricity from head to toe.

Then it happened. The one thing I tried so hard not to do with him because I knew where my heart would go if this happened. We let our emotions take over one night and had sex. Just like I thought, my feelings for Paul grew stronger after that night. Paul felt the same way about me, but there was something holding him back from being with me completely. Paul came from a family with a strong culture that wanted him to marry someone of his descent. You see, Paul was Sikh and he was expected to have an arranged marriage. He had a very strong connection with his family and did everything they told him to do. So, when the conversation came up about where our relationship was headed, it was dead silence. He said to me, "My family will never accept us, and they will disown me if I am with you."

Then came the dagger to my heart as Paul explained to me that he could never be with me completely because I was older, previously married, and had children—the three main things about me that were not going away. These things were a part of me, and he couldn't accept them. The most logical thing to do would have been to stop seeing him and move on with my life, but it wasn't that easy for me—or for us. We both made a choice to continue our relationship even though we knew it was going nowhere. I was desperate to show him that the things preventing us from being together didn't matter, but the harder I tried, the more depressed I felt. I felt like I was robbing myself of my own happiness. It didn't matter how much we loved each other—his family meant everything to him, and he wasn't willing to risk losing them. This created a lot of stress for Paul and me because we wanted to be together so badly and we weren't willing to let go of what we had.

I was so desperate that I agreed to do things with Paul that I didn't want to do. Paul had an addiction to porn, and whenever we were intimate, he had to watch porn. He had his favorite website and porn actress that we would always watch. I felt like I wasn't enough for him, and I always had the question in my head, *Why does he need to watch porn to be turned on? Am I not sexy enough for him? Does my body turn him on? I have these perfect breasts that I paid a lot of money for.*

Then one day the conversation came up about us being with another guy. I had seen this type of sexual intimacy in the porn videos that we watched but never really understood what it was. Paul suggested us doing this on one condition: that it was with his cousin. Deep down, I didn't want to have a sexual relationship with anyone except Paul, but I couldn't lose him, so I agreed to do it. Paul never asked his cousin, and we never went through with it, but the memory of him bringing this up stayed with me. Why would Paul want to share me with anyone if he loved me? This wouldn't be the last time a guy wanted me to have sex with another man in front of him.

It was the summer of 2009. My life felt like a rollercoaster of emotions going nowhere, and I felt myself tumbling down a hill without any way of stopping myself. I was at the end of my rope with my relationship with Paul. I knew that something had to change, but I couldn't figure out how to make it happen. One night, after I got off the phone with Paul, I cried for hours. I felt so much sadness each time I tried to convince Paul that we were meant to be together, and I couldn't understand why he refused to pick me over his family. I couldn't come to terms with the fact that I had given my heart and soul to another man who refused to do the same in return. I felt hopeless, useless, and overwhelmed by the unbearable pain in my body. I was alone in my apartment, sitting at the dining room table in a state of disarray. I was so consumed by my sadness and depression that I let my place go. There was stuff everywhere, totally unorganized. My apartment had become an extension of my thoughts. My life had become too difficult, and I didn't want to live in this world anymore.

I remembered that I had leftover Percocet from when I got my breast implants. I thought that if I took enough of them, I would just fall asleep and not wake up. As I walked to the bathroom to get them, I was crying uncontrollably. Was I really going to go through with this? I had suicidal feelings as a teenager, but I thought I was past all of those feelings. In reality, I wasn't. I grabbed the bottle of Percocet from my medicine cabinet and walked back to my dining room table. I sat down on my hard wooden chair and dumped out the bottle of pills on the table. Still crying uncontrollably, I counted the scattered pills. I thought about my oldest sister who tried to take her life with a bottle of pills. I was a young girl at the time and watched her as she was taken away by the paramedics. My oldest sister didn't die that day. I thought, *What if taking these pills doesn't kill me? Will I be placed in a psychiatric hospital?* My boys wouldn't have their mother anymore.

After staring at the pills on the table for what felt like hours (but it was only minutes), I heard a voice tell me that this wasn't the answer. I thought about my boys and how I wouldn't be able to see them grow up. I would never meet my future grandkids. I thought about that warm summer evening in 1988 when I was sixteen years old and wanted to take my life. How could this be resurfacing in my life after twenty-one years? My Catholic upbringing taught me that suicide is a mortal sin. I picked up the scattered pills on the table and placed them back in the bottle. The next day, I contacted a therapist.

My first therapy session was with a very nice lady. When I arrived at her office, it felt very warm and friendly. As we started talking, she asked general questions to determine a diagnosis and treatment plan. I started to feel more comfortable sharing my life experiences and the reason I was seeking therapy. I don't know why I waited all these years to see a therapist! It felt really good to talk about my feelings, thoughts, and pain with someone who was there for me. I explained that I was overwhelmed with sadness and despair on a daily basis. The feeling of hopelessness and unworthiness didn't seem to go away, and it was worse at night when I was alone and at home.

Then I mustered up the courage to tell the therapist that I felt like disappearing and that I wanted my life to end. I'll never forget what she told me that day. She said to me, "If you take your life, you will break your children." In that moment, I knew that I didn't want my children to be broken. I was broken as a child, and I didn't want my children to go through what I went through. I was determined to change my thinking and break the cycle.

At this point in my life, I knew that something needed to change. I didn't want to feel suicidal anymore—I wanted to live a life full of happiness and joy. Finding a job always came easy for me, and I knew that this would be the first step towards my happiness. I wasn't being challenged at my current job, and I wanted to distance myself from seeing Paul every day, so I contacted the hiring manager who recruited me in the first place. I admired his leadership skills, and the company he joined was doing amazing things and changing the world. He didn't have any opportunities initially, but after a few months of contacting him, something opened up and I was hired. I finally felt like I had a career that no one was going to take away from me.

Self-Love Lesson

"If you have the ability to love, love yourself first."

- Charles Bukowski

10

Trust

"The most terrifying thing is to accept oneself completely."

- C.G. Jung

2009 seemed to fly by, and it finally felt like I was getting my life in order and working towards my inner happiness. Paul and I said our last goodbyes and stopped seeing each other. It was a very difficult goodbye for both of us, but we knew it was the best thing. I was at a point in my life where I was ready for something new, respectful, loving, trusting, and honest. I was still attending therapy sessions, practicing my Buddhism, and cultivating a positive mindset by conditioning my thoughts and reading affirmations daily. I started to surround myself with positive people, and I no longer felt suicidal.

One night while browsing on Facebook, I came across a profile of a guy I knew from high school. His name was Leon. He was the older brother of my first boyfriend—remember Vincent, my first love, the guy who I lost my virginity to and was madly in love with? Only to find out he cheated on me and broke my heart? This guy was Vincent's older brother.

At first, I was just excited to connect with someone familiar and with whom I had a history. I can't recall who friend-requested first, but I remember the first time we talked on the phone. It was as if no time had passed, and we talked for hours, laughing and enjoying the stories from when I was in high school. Leon was the right person I needed to connect with at that stage in my life. He told me that he used to think I was so cute whenever I'd come over to hang out with Vincent. It was kind of odd talking to Vincent's older brother (even though it had been 23 years), but Leon didn't seem to be bothered by the fact that I was with his younger brother at all. In fact, it was as if the relationship between me and his brother didn't exist. Vincent's name didn't come up in our conversation, but I was dying to know how he was doing after all these years. After hours of talking, Leon asked if I wanted to get together for coffee. We both agreed it wasn't a date—just coffee. I accepted the invitation with no expectations other than to start a new friendship and reconnect. At the same time, I was excited that someone I knew asked me out. I couldn't wait to see Leon.

The next day couldn't come fast enough. As I got ready to meet Leon for coffee, many thoughts were running through my head. What if we liked each other? Could we start dating? Would it be awkward since I was with his brother in the past? Would he be different from the other guys? Could I trust him? The nerves were setting in as I headed to Starbucks. When I arrived, he was already there waiting for me. We started walking towards each other, and all I could think of was that I didn't remember him being that short, but boy did he have some muscles. I remember Leon being a muscular guy back then, but he looked even better now. I always told myself I would never date a gym rat, but hey, we weren't dating, right? It was just coffee. As we reached each other, he gave me the tightest hug. We ordered our coffee and hung out for about an hour. We were having a great time. The hour flew by so fast and neither one of us wanted to go home, but it was late and we both had to get up early for work.

As we said our goodbyes, he said to me, "Do you want to go out on a date with me?"

There it was, that word "date." All of the concerns I had about dating him went away, and I said, "Yes, I would love to go on a date with you." I didn't know it then, but saying yes to a date would be the best and worst decision of my life.

Months went by, and Leon and I were growing closer and closer with each passing day. We shared so much of our lives and spent every spare moment we had together. Eventually, we met each other's children, and we couldn't keep our hands off each other. Our relationship was more than just a friendship at this point—we were connected emotionally and spiritually. Our sexual intimacy was unbelievably pleasing. Leon was strong and had a lot of stamina in the bedroom. I think this came from working out all the time at the gym. I didn't care where it came from. All I knew was that he was taking care of me sexually in ways I had never felt before.

One day the conversation came up about me still being married. Both Leon and I could see our future together, and we even talked about marriage. But could I get married again? I had been married twice and failed miserably both times. Maybe third time's a charm? I knew that if I wanted any kind of future, I had to divorce Logan. So, I decided to file for divorce. It was finalized in October 2010.

After Logan and I divorced, Leon and I were able to move forward with our relationship in an honest and trusting way. When I didn't have my boys, I spent the night at Leon's place. He lived with his son, Sam. Eventually, Leon gave me a key to his place since I was there all the time. Pretty soon everyone knew that Leon and I were together. His family found out and was shocked at first because of my relationship with Leon's younger brother in high school. I will never forget the day when I saw Vincent for the first time. I was hanging out at Leon's house, and Vincent came over to visit.

When Vincent arrived, he asked Leon, "Whose car is in the driveway?"

Leon said, "It's Lorrine's car."

Vincent replied, "My Lorrine?"

Wait a minute. Last I checked, I was not *his* Lorrine since high school! I sat on the couch, nervous to see Vincent. I don't even know why I was so nervous, but I could feel my heart beating fast.

The front door started to open and there he was. It was like seeing him for the first time in high school. He looked the same. Handsome as ever, but not a young guy. He was all grown up, a man. A big rush of adrenaline came through me as I stood up and gave him a hug. All of those feelings I had for him in high school came back with that hug—feelings that I didn't know were still there. It was such a rush, and all I could think about was how crazy it was to see him after all these years. When he left, I quickly moved on from those thoughts. I was with Leon, and Vincent was a memory of the past.

By November 2010, Leon and I were living together. Our relationship was moving so fast, but it felt good at the same time. I felt like I had finally found the guy that I would spend the rest of my life with. I trusted and loved him. We not only had a strong bond but we were falling more in love with every passing day. We had a lot in common and got along great. There was no drama in our relationship, and he took care of me.

Everything was perfect until the day I met Leon's ex-wife, Olga, who shared custody of their son, Sam. I had struggled in previous relationships with ex-wives or girlfriends, but this time around, I really wanted to get along with Leon's ex-wife. I knew she would be in his life because they were co-parenting their son, so I set an intention before I met her to get along.

Leon had left the living room for a minute when the doorbell rang. I answered the door and it was Olga and Sam. As I opened the door, Sam said hello and walked to his room. His mom was right behind him. With a smile, I extended my hand to greet her and introduce myself. She looked at me but didn't shake my hand, then she pushed her way past me into the house, hitting me with Sam's bag on her shoulder. I stood in the doorway in shock. I couldn't understand why she was so upset. Later that night, I asked Leon why she would treat me that way, but he didn't know why either. I didn't want to press the issue, so we just dropped it and went to bed.

A few weeks went by before the next encounter with Olga. This time it was worse than the first time. It was a weekend she had Sam, and Leon and I were hanging out at home enjoying a quiet evening to ourselves. We decided to go to bed early. Normally, we take our cell phones into the bedroom with us, but on this night, Leon left his cell phone in the living room. The next morning when we woke up, Leon had several missed calls and text messages from Olga. He had a look of worry on his face when I asked him what Olga wanted.

He said, "Her car broke down and she was asking me to come help her."

Confused at what he was saying, I asked him, "Doesn't she have a boyfriend? Why couldn't he come help her?"

Neither of us knew why she contacted him instead of her boyfriend. He called her back, but I didn't hear the conversation because he went outside to talk to her. I tried to remain calm and positive, and I did my best not to get involved. This was Leon's situation, and it was best for me to stay out of it.

Later that afternoon, Olga was supposed to drop Sam off. She arrived on time, but instead of just dropping him off, she came up to the door. Leon and I were sitting on the couch as she walked in behind Sam. Standing with her arms crossed and a stern posture in the doorway, she said to us in a condescending tone, "I'm glad you both are here because what I have to say is for both of you." We both sat quietly as she proceeded to say, "When I called Leon, I expected him to come help me and his son."

I could feel my emotions starting to overtake my calmness. "We were sleeping," I said, "and we didn't hear your call or text." I started feeling angry that she would even expect him to come to her aid, so I proceeded to say, "Don't you have a boyfriend to help you?"

Well, this pissed her off, and she said to me, "Why would I call him if Leon is closer."

I stood up, walked directly in front of her, and said, "You need to leave now."

"I'm not leaving."

"Yes, you are," I said as I moved closer to her.

Neither of us were backing down. Leon could see the tension building up as he stood up and stopped us from arguing any further. Olga eventually did back down, but not without grumbling and threatening to take Sam away from Leon. I allowed my anger to get the best of me, and I was so upset that I couldn't make out what she was saying as she left. The last thing I said to her was, "We will see you in court," as she slammed the door.

Leon was just as upset as I was. By this time, I was crying and mostly upset at myself for acting the way I did. I wanted to talk to Leon about it, but he wasn't having it. He told me that I shouldn't have said anything to her, then he grabbed his car keys and left. There I stood, crying and confused as to what just happened. Leon was gone for a few hours and finally came back home. I was already lying in bed but I couldn't sleep. He came into the bedroom and didn't say a word to me. He just changed out of his clothes and went straight to bed. This was the first time I'd seen Leon this way. As I lay in bed, replaying everything in my head, I still couldn't wrap my mind around it all. Leon and Olga had been divorced for quite some time before I came into the picture. He had told me that they got along great for the benefit of their son, but that it was definitely over between the two of them. Why then was she so territorial over Leon, and why did he take her side in this situation? We were a couple building our lives together, and he should have protected my feelings rather than his ex-wife's. But instead, he left me standing there crying and came home with nothing more to say.

All these thoughts came crashing down on me like a big tidal wave. Did I make a mistake again and move in with a guy who didn't have my best interests at heart? Crying silently, I eventually fell asleep—but what came in the coming months would be a testament of my strength.

As the months went by, I started to discover some concerning things. One night, I came home and walked into a huge amount of papers and envelopes laying everywhere in the living room. It looked like a tornado had ripped through. The house was dark, and no one was home. My initial reaction was, *Did someone break in? Where are Leon and Sam?*

I was calling out for Leon, but there was no answer. Just dead silence. Then I walked towards the bedrooms and looked inside Sam's room. His bed was turned upside down and everything was in shambles. It looked just like the living room. I picked up my cell phone to call Leon. His phone went straight to voicemail, so I texted him, "I'm home and the place is a mess. I'm worried. Where are you? Please call me." Thirty minutes went by with no answer. Frantic, I called his phone again and again and again. Still no answer. Straight to voicemail. I didn't know what to do. Nothing appeared to be missing, but I wasn't sure if I should call the police anyway. I just sat and waited for Leon to call me back or come home.

Finally, hours later, Leon pulled into the driveway. His face looked like someone had just died. I asked him what happened to the house.

"Why is everything thrown everywhere?" I demanded. "And what happened to Sam's room?"

He stood there and said, "It's nothing, I don't want to talk about it."

If Leon didn't want to talk about things, we wouldn't talk about it. Confused and upset, I didn't ask anything more as we both started to clean up the mess.

This was just one of Leon's episodes of rage. His anger and depression continued for months. Leon had bouts of rage, and each time I dismissed it. I made excuses for him and thought he was just having a bad day. Then I realized—it wasn't just a bad day. He was happy one moment, and within minutes, his mood would change. One time his dog didn't listen to him and while she was in her cage, he picked up the cage and threw it out onto the patio. We got into an argument one time, and I fell to the ground and he almost punched me in the face. Another time, we were at the car dealership test-driving cars for him. The salesman wanted to test drive his current car to make sure that if we did a trade-in, the car was in working condition. According to Leon, the salesman peeled out of the parking lot, and when he returned, Leon started yelling and cussing at him in front of everyone at the dealership. Other times he would just sit in the dark living room and not say anything to me for hours.

There was no communication between the two of us, and I started to doubt whether this relationship was going to last. I loved Leon and I wanted our relationship to work, but I felt helpless trying to figure out what was wrong. Not only that, but trying to get along with Olga was exhausting and put me on an emotional rollercoaster. One minute we got along and the next we hated each other. Leon and I started arguing more about it—he always took her side and said that I was the troublemaker. I was determined to find out why he was so protective of her and always took her side, so I started snooping around. I know, I should have trusted him, but the truth is, I didn't. I thought if I could find some evidence of what my intuition was telling me about Leon and his ex-wife, I would feel better about leaving him.

One night as he slept, I got up and went to check his cell phone. He never wanted me to have his password and was always secretive with his phone. But I covertly watched him unlock his phone one day and memorized his phone password. As I unlocked his phone, my hands were trembling, afraid he would wake up and catch me. I clicked on his text messages, specifically looking for texts to Olga. There it was—a long history of text messages to her. Some were normal and about their son, but then I came across one that sent. It said, "Was those new jeans you were wearing the other day?" She said, "Yes, do you like my butt?" He said, "Yes, you have always had a nice butt." Then I scrolled further and found more flirtatious text messages, and the flirting went both ways. I know it was just text messages, but I couldn't help but wonder what else he was hiding from me. Clearly, their relationship was more than just co-parenting like he portrayed it to be. I was determined to find more, so I checked his call log. What could he possibly be talking to her about every day at the same time? My heart sank. My intuition was right. I decided not to say anything right away and waited to see what else I would discover.

The next day I came home early and found the password to his online account for his cell phone bill. I wanted to show him proof that I knew about his frequent daily calls with Olga, so I logged on and printed out the statements for a few months of cell phone bills. I highlighted her number on the bill over a hundred times. As I sat there highlighting, I was getting more and more upset. I couldn't hold in my emotions anymore, so when he got home that night, I confronted him. I showed him the copies with her number highlighted and asked him about the flirtatious text messages to her.

He was furious that I went through his cell phone and looked at his phone bills without his permission.

He yelled at me and said, "You are causing trouble. Olga is Sam's mother, and I have to talk to her." I said to him, "Every day and around the same time? What could you two be talking about that requires you to speak every day at the same time?" Just like all of our other arguments, he became quiet and stormed away, leaving me in tears. As I watched him walk away once again, I couldn't help but think about my previous failed marriages and how pathetic I was to allow myself to be in another relationship that didn't serve me. I cried myself to sleep that night with pain in my heart. Despite how upset I was, I was desperate to show Leon how much I loved him. I wasn't going to lose him to another woman—I was going to fight with every last bone I had in my body.

Self-Love Lesson

"You can be the most beautiful person in the world and everybody sees light and rainbows when they look at you, but if you yourself don't know it, all of that doesn't even matter. Every second that you spend on doubting your worth, every moment that you use to criticize yourself, is a second of your life wasted, is a moment of your life thrown away. It's not like you have forever, so don't waste any of your seconds, don't throw even one of your moments away."

- C. JoyBell C.

11

Third Times A Charm

"If you ignore the red flags, embrace the heartache to come."

- Amanda Mosher

In February 2011, I decided to move out of Leon's place. I thought if we didn't live together, maybe we could make our relationship work. We had only been living together for three months, and our problems were growing larger by the day. They say absence makes the heart grow fonder, and at first, it seemed to be working. Our arguments diminished, and we were getting along great. It was just like when we first met, but I missed being with Leon every day. I didn't miss the arguments and ex-wife jealousy stuff, of course, but I missed being in his arms.

Was it his arms that I missed, or was it just me settling for anyone who would hold me again? I always hated being alone, and whenever my boys were not with me, all I could think about was Leon. I had my own place, but I spent the night at Leon's house three or four times a week and every other weekend. We both knew that not living together was definitely helping our relationship, but at the same time, we missed each other when we were not together. So, in May 2011, I moved back in with him.

I know what you're thinking. Why would someone move out just to move back in? Trust me, I thought it was a crazy move also, but I still had deep desperation to win Leon over his ex-wife. I just didn't want another failed relationship. Instead of focusing on myself and my needs, I decided to put all my energy into Leon and our relationship. I would soon discover more heartache.

The first few weeks back with Leon were unbelievably good. We were still getting along great, and I even decided to make amends with Olga. I knew if I wanted Leon and me to work, I would have to get along with Olga, so I took a different approach with her. I decided to befriend her, and I even took it further by including her in my daily affirmations and sending her positive inspirational messages in the morning. Everything seemed to be going great and we were all getting along well until Leon and I shared our exciting news. No, we were not expecting a baby—but we were to soon be Mr. and Mrs. Leon!

One day while hanging out, Leon and I started talking about if something happened to either one of us, we would want each other to take care of our affairs. I suggested that we list each other as a beneficiary on our insurances. Leon thought it was a good idea but then said to me, "Why don't we just get married?"

I said to him, "Really?"

He said, "Why not?"

The desperation of being alone popped into my mind and without hesitation, I said, "Yes, I will marry you."

It was the most unromantic conventional proposal ever. He didn't even have a wedding ring or get down on one knee in a romantic setting, but I said yes anyway. I won Leon over his ex-wife, and he would finally take my side as I was soon to be his wife.

I don't know if we both thought we would die tomorrow, but we picked a quick wedding date and got married in June 2011. We both decided not to let our children know right away—instead, we would tell them when the time was right. I think we both knew it was too soon and we didn't want them to be upset. But in the back of my mind, I wondered if his reasoning was not to upset his ex-wife. Yes, I still had insecure feelings about him and Olga, but I chose to ignore these feelings. My intuition was telling me not to marry this guy, but I didn't think anyone else would want me, so I settled.

We had a small wedding with only his sister and parents. We didn't have a reception, but we planned to have one when we got back from our honeymoon where we would announce to our family and friends that we were married. We booked a trip to Maui and had a great time. No arguments or ex-wife distractions. It truly felt like our relationship was headed in the right direction, but I still felt like I couldn't trust him. I couldn't forget about what I discovered on his cell phone and his pattern of non-communication whenever we got into arguments. Here I was on our honeymoon, doubting our relationship. What was wrong with me? Had I made a mistake again?

Weeks after our wedding and honeymoon, we started planning our wedding reception. We decided it was time to let our children know with the exception of my two youngest boys. We called each child and told them. They all seemed happy for us, but I could hear the curiosity in their voices as to why we were telling only them. One of his kids asked about the wedding and why they were not invited. We really didn't have an answer other than it was small, short, and sweet. Then the day of our wedding reception finally arrived. All of our friends and family were there. It was a good time, and we all felt a lot of joy that day. Leon and I were glowing with happiness.

But it wasn't long after our wedding reception when I started noticing that Leon was struggling with his finances and paying his bills. I helped out where I could, and I paid my portion of the rent, but I don't think it was enough. Before long, Leon's behavior started to change and was almost on a daily basis. One moment he was happy, loving, and laughing with me. The next moment he was depressed, angry, and quiet, with no engagement or communication with me.

I tried not to let his behavior affect me, but it was hard living with someone who went through so many mood swings. I wasn't used to being around this type of behavior before, and I wasn't sure how to live with it. But nevertheless, I was determined to make him a happy husband and was willing to do anything for him. I thought if I could just find out what made him happy, he would love me more and we would live happily ever after.

One night after having sex, we started talking about sexual fantasies. I really didn't have any to share, and I asked him what his was. He proceeded to tell me that he would love to see me have sex with another man in front of him. At first, I was in shock that my own husband would want me to have sex with another man—and in front of him, no less! Why would he want to share me with another man? Remember Paul wanting me to have sex with him and his cousin? I couldn't help but wonder if I had manifested this into my relationship with Leon . . .

He said that it would turn him on if I would do this for him. I wanted him to love me and please him sexually, so I agreed to do it. The next day while I was at work, I received a text from Leon. It was a picture of a fully-naked guy with an erect penis and a text that read, "What do you think about this one?" I immediately called him to ask what the picture was about. He said to me it was a guy he found in an online advertisement looking for sex. In my head, I thought *Wow! Leon is really going for what we talked about.* It was all happening so fast. I didn't know what to say—I didn't want to comment on another guy's body because I was afraid Leon would get upset with me, so I said to him that if he thought it was good, we should go for it.

By the time I got home that evening, Leon had already made a date with for us to get together with this guy. In the days leading up to this sexual encounter with a strange man, my nerves were high and kept saying to myself, *Am I really going to go through with this?* But it's what Leon wanted, and if this would make him happy, I was willing to give my body to another man for him.

The weekend finally arrived when we would be meeting sexual encounter #1. Leon organized the entire night. We were to meet this guy at his place. I was very skeptical about meeting at someone's place we didn't know, but Leon assured me there was nothing to be concerned about. He had vetted this guy and he assured me he was not going to do anything to harm us. I didn't know what to wear, so I asked Leon.

He said, "Wear something sexy and revealing. I want these guys to desire you from the moment you walk in the door."

I found a form-fitting short black skirt and low-cut blouse in my closet, with three-inch black strappy stiletto sandals. As I got dressed, I started visualizing what would happen once we arrived at this guy's house. I visualized Leon being so turned on that it would be an experience we both would not forget. Little did I know that this would not be the last—and that it would lead me down a dark path I could not escape.

As we headed to the guy's house, we both were excited with curiosity. I had only seen this guy's penis picture and didn't know what he looked like. Leon assured me that I would think he was attractive. But to be honest, I didn't care about what this guy looked like—it wasn't like we were going to date. It was purely a one-time sexual experience that would be over in a couple of hours. We finally arrived at the house. It was a nice, big house from the outside. As we rang the doorbell, my hands were clammy and sweaty, so when the guy answered the door, I didn't shake his hand. The inside of his house was very nice. He asked us if we wanted a glass of wine. I quickly responded with a yes. I needed to calm my nerves and I knew alcohol would do the trick. After about thirty minutes getting to know each other in the kitchen, we were led into the back where his bedroom was. It was dark but glowing with candles.

As I stood there in the dark, nervous about what would happen next, I felt someone behind me. There was a warm breath on my skin as I felt a wet kiss on my neck. This stranger took my hand and guided me to the bed where he slowly lay me down and gently kissed the inside of my thighs up to my vagina. Leon lay next to me on the bed, kissing my lips and caressing my breasts with his hands. As Leon unbuttoned my blouse, the guy started to remove my panties and my skirt. Leon handed him a condom. The guy put the condom on and got on top of me, thrusting himself inside me for a few minutes. Then he turned me over and pulled me up on my knees, thrusting himself behind me while Leon stood in front of me as I was pleasuring him with my mouth. They were so turned on that they both ejaculated within minutes of each other, and it was over. As we all got dressed, the guy asked if we would be interested in doing this again. Confused by the question, I didn't answer. I agreed to this as a one-time experience. Leon answered for us and told the guy we would let him know.

On the way home, Leon asked me if I liked what just happened and if I wanted to do it again. I was at a loss for words. I wanted Leon to be happy, and I didn't want our marriage to fail, so I agreed—not knowing what the effects would be on my soul. All I cared about was making Leon happy and staying married. The thought of going through another divorce and breakup would be too shameful and embarrassing for me to bear.

When we arrived home that night, I needed to take a shower. I felt like I was covered in filth. As I stood in the warm water, I started to cry. My husband was okay with sharing me, and I was ashamed of what I'd done.

The next day at work was a blur. I couldn't focus—all I could do was worry and wonder when Leon would ask me to do this again. I left early and headed home. When I arrived home, Leon was still at work. I wanted to do something to take my mind off the sexual encounter, so I decided to browse the internet and shop. Shopping always took my mind off things.

I used our home computer, and when I logged on, Leon's email was up on the screen. I wasn't going to look, but my curiosity always got the best of me. I saw the emails he was sending to these guys about getting together with us. One particular email caught my eye as the subject line read, "What I sent him." I clicked on it and there was an email from Leon to a guy that read, "Hello and good morning. Pleasure setting will be about pleasing my wife. It's all about her that evening. She doesn't like rough stuff, no anal or anything crazy. You can enjoy her as much as she wants you to. Me, I'm not the jealous type. I can just sit back and watch you two go at it. I can jump in once in a while. It's all up to her. Can you reply from your personal email and send your contact number? Also, can you send more pictures of your face? Let's get to know each other before we surprise her. Thanks."

As I read this, I started to feel like Leon wasn't just doing this for pleasure and fantasy anymore. Based on what I was reading, it seemed like he had another plan for our sex life and it included other men. I started to think, "Is he gay?" Does he want to be with another man, or does he enjoy seeing men have sex with me? Then I thought, *Maybe he doesn't feel like he can satisfy me.* All of these thoughts racing through my head was driving me crazy. He was emailing these random guys, and I didn't know he was doing it. I didn't want to read anymore, so I logged out of his email. I sat in silence, full of hurt, confusion, and despair. I knew if I brought it up to Leon, we would get into an argument, so I decided not to say anything.

A couple of weeks after our first sexual encounter with the first random guy, Leon approached me with the idea again. He said that he'd found another guy who was interested in joining us in the bedroom. My mind was filled with so much confusion, and I could feel my voice wanting to scream from the top of my lungs that I didn't want to do this anymore. I wanted to ask him why he was emailing these guys without my knowledge and planning hook-ups. But I was so afraid of the consequences that nothing came out of my mouth. All I could hear is the sound of my voice saying to him, "Ok."

Later that week, it was a beautiful Friday afternoon. I always loved Fridays because it was time to relax and enjoy the weekend with Leon. I was praying that Leon had forgotten about the idea of getting together with another guy and we would go somewhere fun just the two of us this weekend. I arrived home to find Leon waiting for me in the living room. He seemed more anxious than normal. He said excitedly, "The guy confirmed and will meet us tonight."

Very surprised, I said to him, "Where will he meet us? I need to get ready."

Leon said, "Don't worry about the details. Just jump in the shower and I will work everything else out."

I hopped in the shower, and as I was lathering my body with my loofah, I heard the bathroom door open. Then the shower curtain opened and standing there was a naked guy—some random stranger that I didn't know. I was given no formal introduction or even his name. Leon was right behind him and said, "This is the guy I was telling you about." The guy got into the shower with me and took the loofah from me. He stood behind me and started to rub my body up and down as he caressed my breasts and vagina with his hands. Leon had left the bathroom and was waiting for us in the bedroom. I was so uncomfortable showering with this strange man and Leon not being there, so I told him, "I'm going to get out now." I wrapped myself in a towel as he followed me to the bedroom. Leon was on the bed, naked, waiting for us.

Leon called me to the bed and told me not to put any clothes on. The guy was right behind me. I lay down next to Leon and the guy lay next to me so that I was between them. It was as if the entire situation was planned—only I wasn't part of the planning. Leon started to kiss me and pull me towards him. The guy started to caress my breasts from behind and pushed himself up against me. I could feel his hard penis pressing against my naked body. Then Leon turned me on my back and told the guy to get on top of me. He got on top and started to slide his penis inside of me as Leon was kissing and sucking on my breasts. Then I heard the guy say, "I'm going to cum," and it was over. These encounters always ended quicker than they started. No words, no small talk, no cuddling with each other. The guy simply said goodbye and left.

I lay in the bed that I had considered to be Leon's and my sacred space, but now it had been defiled. He had invited another man into our bedroom, and there was no going back now. My body was numb with sadness and loss. I felt my soul leaving my body. I wanted to be someone else so that I could go back to the way things used to be.

Self-Love Lesson

"Some of us were made to believe that you need a man, or a woman, to be happy. I say you need to know yourself and love yourself to find that elusive emotion that we call happiness."

- Hagir Elsheikh

12

Losing My Soul

*"He brought out the worst in me, and was
the best thing that ever happened to me."*

- Coco J. Ginger

I started to slip into a deep depression after the second sexual encounter. I wasn't doing the things that I loved anymore. I gave up practicing my Buddhism or going to therapy because I thought I had "found my happy" with Leon and I didn't need to work on myself anymore. But all the while, my intuition was telling me that something was not right. We had only been married for four months, and already it felt like our marriage was failing. I blamed myself for what was happening. A lot of should-haves were running through my head. I should have respected myself more and told Leon that having sex with another man made me feel disrespected and unloved. I should have spoken up and told Leon how I felt about everything. But I just couldn't get past my fear of being alone and having another failed marriage. I felt desperate, and I was running out of options. My inner critic kept saying: *You're getting old and no one will want you, especially after three marriages and being a single mother of four boys.* So I allowed my body to be given to these random men despite how it made me feel each time.

Pretty soon, our sex life was non-existent unless we were with strangers. Leon didn't get sexually turned on with just the two of us, and he needed to have another man join us in the bedroom to get aroused. It became a necessity instead of a fantasy for him. Every other weekend, Leon planned another sexual encounter and wouldn't share the plan with me. One time, he invited a guy to our house and told me that he was going to give me a relaxing massage. That's not all he did—after the massage, Leon wanted me to have sex with him while he watched. Just like the good wife that I was, I did what Leon wanted me to do.

The next morning as I was cleaning up the kitchen, I started thinking about why these random guys would want to have sex with me and Leon. I believed it was for their own sexual gratification, but I felt like there was something more to the encounters. Then it dawned on me. Leon was always the one to talk to these guys and coordinated all of the sexual encounters. I didn't have these guy's numbers, names, or emails. Leon had everything. What was the exchange he was doing with these men? It felt like there was a lock and chain attached to my heart, pulling me down to the deepest part of my soul. I know that Leon was challenged with his finances, but would he really be doing something so deceitful and demoralizing to our relationship as getting men to pay to have sex with me? I mean, he was already asking me to do the unbelievable act of having sex with these men while he watched or joined in. What could be more demoralizing than this? I didn't know what to believe anymore. I had reached a point of no return.

I lost myself once again and hit rock bottom. No, I wasn't an alcoholic, but I could only imagine what it feels like to be in that dark place. I felt like I hit my rock bottom in loving someone. I was exhausted and knew that something had to change in my life. I knew that I had to get out of this relationship or it would ruin me. Even if Leon and I talked about trying to make it work, I would never be able to trust him. Somehow, I thought that if we got married, all of these issues would go away and we would have a happy, loving, honest relationship. I saw all the red flags early on in our relationship but chose to ignore them. I wanted Leon to be happy and would do anything to make it happen, even if it caused my own unhappiness.

Here I was, once again in a relationship that didn't serve me or my happiness. I deserved to be happy, but why couldn't I get there? I felt unworthy and in a dark place in my mind, body, and soul. What was preventing me from finding my true happiness? Why did I keep attracting the same guys in my life? Deep down I felt like I knew what I needed to do, but I had no idea how to do it. I knew that I wanted to finally get out of attracting these types of men who didn't respect me and didn't have my best interests at heart. I wanted to find my true happiness, and even though I was going through this tough time, I didn't give up on love. The only way I was going to find what I was seeking in my life was to be on my own and take a break from dating.

I needed a plan on where I was going to live. I relied on Leon for my living situation; I knew that I needed to start looking for a place to live first. I started to do inner work and build up the strength and courage to get out of this relationship. I started to practice my Buddhism again by chanting. I had nowhere to put up my altar, and

Leon didn't support my practice, so I chanted to myself whenever I could. I purchased self-help books on how to love yourself and subscribed to positive newsletters. I dived into whatever was going to help build my confidence, courage, and strength to leave.

There is a favorite quote of mine, "The ocean stirs the heart, inspires the imagination, and brings eternal joy to the soul." I always loved the ocean and knew it was my happy place. I wanted to get far away from Leon and heal, so I decided to lease an apartment near the beach. I had no friends in this small beach town, but my intuition was telling me that this was the right thing to do. I found a perfect two-bedroom apartment one block from the ocean. I could see the ocean from my back patio. It was truly magical, and I felt right at home as soon as I opened the front door. I knew Leon wasn't going to let me go easily, so I signed the lease and scheduled a move-in date while Leon was at work. I wrote him a note, left it on the coffee table, and moved out in April 2012. I was finally free from the silence of my own voice, and I was determined to find myself and true happiness.

Just as I suspected, Leon was furious with me when he arrived home and saw the note. The nasty, degrading emails and text messages started to arrive. I knew that I had to stay strong and not get dragged back into his drama, but even after all of the heartache, I felt bad for him. I never wanted to hurt him. I left to find my own happiness. I filed for divorce, and it was final in September 2012.

After my divorce from Leon, I did some serious soul-searching. Every night I walked or jogged to the ocean, and I found my favorite piece of driftwood that I would sit on. I would always listen to love songs when I was sad or going through a breakup, and in some strange way, the songs brought out the feelings I was holding in and I was able to release them into the Universe. I was determined to forgive Leon and everyone who had hurt me in the past, including myself, so that I could move on. Going to the ocean every day brought out a lot of pain and heartache I was holding inside of me. At the same time, the ocean was healing my heart.

I remember one day while walking on the beach, I heard a song on my playlist called Jar of Hearts by Christina Perri. As I listened to this song, I thought about all of my failed relationships and how my heart was always in a jar waiting to be released. From this day forward, I vowed to take care of my heart. First thing every morning, I would read positive affirmations about self-love. I hung them on my bathroom mirror because I knew I wouldn't miss reading it in this place. It looked like positive affirmations exploded all over my place! I hung them everywhere to remind myself whenever I started to go back to that dark place. I was determined to break the cycle and not attract the same type of guy anymore. I wanted to attract a healthy, loving, honest, trustworthy man. More importantly, I wanted to love myself because I knew that I couldn't love anyone until I loved myself. One of my favorite self-love affirmations is by Louise Hay: "I flow freely and lovingly with life. I love myself. I know that only good awaits me at every turn."

Three months after leaving Leon, I started to feel better about myself and where my life was headed. Then, one day at work, I was talking with a man named Mario, who was a manager of a group that I supported. He was always wound-up and stressed out. He was notorious for complaining, and he always had a negative vibe to him. Mario didn't have any qualities of the type of guy I was looking for, so I thought he would be a safe person to befriend. I also wanted to help him see the positive side of life. Mario mentioned that he lived in the same town as me, so I suggested we carpool to work sometimes. Not knowing where this would lead, he agreed, and we started to carpool.

At first, it was just carpool buddies, then the texting started at work—and eventually after work. I really thought it was just going to be a friendship that we were developing, but I was naive to think that's all it would be. I was very attracted to him, and he was attracted to me. I didn't want to believe that this attraction would go anywhere, but it was stronger than both of our wills. One caveat to this attraction—he was married. I know what you're thinking. Not again, Lorrine! Didn't you learn your lesson with the previous affairs with married or unavailable men? You were supposed to be healing your heart and soul. Loving yourself enough to attract the right man. Well, I still had a lesson to learn. I felt lonely, craving that feeling to be loved. Here was an attractive man wanting to give this to me, and everything that I was trying to do for my life went out the window. Again.

I was trying to justify this relationship in my head because I had worked hard to find myself and happiness. Mario told me that he wasn't happy in his marriage and that he was trying to figure out a way to leave his wife, but he had two small children and didn't want to hurt them. I believed him, so one day after work, I invited him into my place for a glass of wine. I knew it wasn't going to just be a glass of wine. As soon as we opened the door, we couldn't keep our hands off each other and had sex. After he left to go home to his wife, I felt horrible inside. What had I done?

Our affair went on for a couple of months. Mario would come over early before work to have sex with me, then we would carpool to work. It wasn't too often that he would come over after work, because he was always in a rush to get home to his family. I don't know why I was so upset when he would leave me after having sex and not stay the night. I knew what I was getting into, and I should have expected all of this to happen. He was a married man, and I was the mistress who gave him sex. I allowed my body to once again become an object for sexual pleasure.

After three months of this routine, I ended the affair. He had no plans to leave his wife and family, and I wanted him to do what made him happy. I knew what it felt like to be cheated on and undervalued. I wanted the bad karma to end, and I wasn't willing to continue a relationship with an unavailable guy. I deserved to be treated better. I deserved to be with someone who was honest and available, both emotionally and physically. After I ended the relationship with Mario, I realized how much I respected my body and the internal love I had for myself was growing stronger. Leaving Leon to find myself and heal at my happy place was the best thing that ever happened to me. I would have never ended the relationship with Mario and would have continued to stay in a relationship that didn't serve me if I hadn't learned to love myself. I was finally in a place where I made decisions on what was best for me and my happiness. I was no longer in a place of fear. I was prioritizing myself. I set healthy boundaries for myself and trusted the process of my heart healing.

Everything was feeling good in my life. I was living a block from my happy place, the ocean, and I was finding myself more each day. Then I received a phone call from my second ex-husband, Logan. He had met a girl and was moving back to the area to live with her. I was over-the-top excited to hear the news because my boys would be closer to me and I wouldn't have to drive them home so far away every other weekend. I also would be getting them more often, and also during the week, which made me super happy but stressed at the same time. The drive to their school would still be an hour away, which would mean they had to wake up early so that I could get them to school on time. This put a lot of strain on the boys and me. I wanted to stay where I was living so bad, and I tried to make it work. My soul was happy here, but it was tough on the boys, and I knew that I had to sacrifice my happiness for theirs. I was happy where my kids were, and I was going to live the rest of my life for them. There is a beautiful quote by Shannon L. Alder, "Blessed is a mother that would give up part of her soul for her children's happiness."

After one school year of doing this drive, I decided to leave the beach town and move to the same town as their dad. This decision brought me a lot of sadness, and I promised myself that after the boys graduated high school, I would move back one day. I started my apartment search and affirmed that we would find the right place to live. I pulled an affirmation from my Power Thought Card Deck by Louise Hay, hung it on my bathroom mirror, and affirmed every day. It was an affirmation for finding a home: "I see myself living in a wonderful place. It fulfills all of my needs and desires. It's in a beautiful location and at a price I can afford."

Well, I did find the perfect place, less than fifteen minutes away from my ex-husband and the boy's school. The moving truck arrived, and all the boxes were loaded. As we drove away from the beach, I could feel a part of my soul being left behind. Quietly, I whispered to my soul and said, "You are on the right path now. Don't worry, you will be back one day."

Self-Love Lesson:

"Every woman that finally figured out her worth, has picked up her suitcases of pride and boarded a flight to freedom, which landed in the valley of change."

- Shannon L. Alder

Reflecting back on this third part of my life, all of these lessons have taught me one of the biggest things—and that is to have a voice. I learned that not having a voice and not speaking up only put me in situations that I didn't want to be in. I grew up in an environment where I wasn't taught how to love myself. I wasn't told as a child (or as a teenager) that I was beautiful just the way I was. I carried feelings of unworthiness into my adulthood, and I thought if I could change my body, I would be happier. The truth is, the breast augmentation didn't make me happier. Maybe for a brief moment in time, it satisfied that desire of loving my body, but eventually, that desire burned out inside me and I was back to feeling unworthy and unattractive. The negative inner critic came out in me, which made me more depressed.

I didn't realize what I was doing to my soul until my friend introduced me to positive affirmations and putting out to the Universe what

I wanted in life. At first, I struggled with the concept of saying positive affirmations out loud. Even saying to myself, "I love you," was a challenge. No matter how hard the challenges were, I pushed through it and every day got easier to affirm what I wanted. My first husband George getting deported was not the easiest thing to accept. I was a single mother and still couldn't give my kids the love and attention they needed. I was broken inside. Sending my son Romeo at the age of thirteen to live with my mother was the hardest yet the best thing I have ever done. My mother raised him to be a responsible and honest man. My mother wasn't the best role model for me, but she was different with the grand-kids. She loved and wanted the best for them. I will never understand why my mother couldn't be there for me growing up, but I will be forever thankful to her for raising my son.

Even though I was affirming and working on myself, I still couldn't get past the fear of being alone. I felt like I wasn't whole and complete without a man by my side. With every guy I met, I always thought he was "The One." But in reality, I settled time and time again. When I met Paul, it felt amazing, but then we had to keep our relationship a secret from the world. The addictions he had to pornography made me feel less of a woman, but it wasn't really the pornography that made me feel that way. I was responsible for my own happiness, and I should not have tried to change Paul for who he was. I had a choice to stay in the relationship. I stayed even though I knew the ramifications of making this decision.

With every failed relationship, I slipped further into depression. I didn't want to live anymore, and I had constant thoughts of suicide. Almost taking my life in my 30s was a wake-up call for me. I thought my kids would be better off without me and my broken spirit until a therapist told me the point-blank truth. I will never forget what she told me: "You will break your children if you take your life." She saved my life that day. I didn't want my children to be broken like I was, and thankfully suicide never crossed my mind again. I finally had a career I could call my own, and no one was going to take it away from me. Practicing Buddhism brought back the joy and light into my world. I really felt like my life was heading in the right direction—until I met Leon.

I thought I was going to spend the rest of my life with Leon. I didn't want to have another failed relationship. But once again, I was in a relationship where I was trying to change the person I was with. I wanted him to love me so desperately that I sacrificed my own happiness and voice for his happiness. I thought that marrying Leon would make our relationship stronger. I wanted him to choose me over his ex-wife, and I would do anything to win his love. The truth is, I didn't know the man I was marrying, and competing with his ex-wife was juvenile. I made excuses for his narcissistic behavior and domination over me. After marrying him, I found out that he had a cuckold fantasy. Surprisingly, there is a large number of heterosexual married men who have cuckold fantasies. I thought this would be a one-time thing, but it soon became a part of this regular fantasy, and I played the part of the hot wife. He was the cuck. For those of you who don't know what cuckold fantasy is, let me explain. I had to google this term myself.

According to Dr. Justin Lehmiller, a cuckold fantasy is the man finds the prospect of watching their wives have sex with other guys to be sexually arousing. There are many reasons why a man would want to do this with his wife, but after the first time doing this with Leon, I didn't want it anymore. I didn't have the voice, courage, or strength to tell him, and each time we did this, my soul was stripped from me. Leon passed away in April 2020. I will never know the reason why he had the cuckold fantasy and can only speculate the reasoning. We parted on bad terms, and I will never be able to apologize for the hurt I caused him by leaving the way I did. I forgave Leon for all the hurt he caused me, and I believe that he was placed into my life to make me stronger. If it wasn't for him, I would have never found my voice and reclaimed my soul. I learned how to love myself, and I figured out what I wanted in my life to make me happy.

Self-Love Lesson

*"In the journey of finding love,
I focus on loving myself first."*

~ Angel Moreira

Part Four

13

Freeing Your Heart For Love

"Love recognizes no barriers. It jumps, hurdles, leaps, fences, penetrates walls to arrive at its destination full of hope."

- Maya Angelou

What is love? This is a question I asked myself for twenty-nine years. I thought I knew what love was. I had so much love to give, but it felt like I was never going to find love. I wanted to be loved. Not just to be loved by someone but to feel it in my mind, body, and soul. With every breakup, I found myself jumping right back into the same type of relationship with a different guy. I loved hard and would do anything these guys wanted me to do just to get their love in return, even if it meant hurting myself. My body became their temple for lust, adultery, and sexual attraction. Unavailable guys were only attracted to me for sex. They were not in love with me; they were in lust with me. I didn't know the difference, and I often combined the two into one.

When I did find someone who was emotionally available, he would cheat on me. It was like walking on a knife's edge, and each time I would fall, my heart would slice open and hurt even more.

Then I thought of my karma, because I believed in cause and effect. According to the World Tribune, "Nichiren Buddhism teaches that the law of cause and effect is simultaneous. At the exact time that we make a cause, the effect is created." Was it my karma because I had a relationship with a married man? I remember one of the many therapists I saw tell me, "Sometimes your heart has to break wide open before you can experience what true love is." I cried hysterically that night, asking myself, "Why *my* heart? What did I do to deserve this?" I was a good person, and all I ever wanted was to live a happy and loving life. The problem is, I didn't know what love was. Heck, I didn't even know how to love myself yet. How could someone possibly love me if I couldn't love myself first? I suffered from heartache, pain, loss, confusion, and depression. In my mind, I had no directions, and I lost my way with no way back to the path.

A wise person once told me that people come in and out of your life for a reason. Now, twenty-nine years later, I know why I had to experience all of the hurt and suffering. I was a vehicle to share my story. Some people live their entire lives not knowing or feeling what true happiness or love feels like. You don't have to be that person. Through the power of positive thinking, affirmations, and visualizing what you want in life, you can find what you are truly seeking in your mind, body, and soul. I found my true happiness, purpose, and passion, but most of all, I found self-love. I hope to encourage people who are going through difficult challenges in their life that they can and will find their happiness. It will just take hard work, determination, and willpower to get there. They will have to do all the work to find happiness and self-love. But they will get there.

I was obsessed with love-story movies, and thought if I watched them, I too could have that kind of love. I had one guy tell me,

"Love is not a fairytale or a movie." Maybe he was right, but I still dreamed of finding a movie kind of love—and I knew that if I put it out to the Universe, it would come to me at the right time. I have many favorites, but my all-time favorite movie is *The Notebook*. I would watch this movie over and over again. I even purchased the DVD, but if it even played on TV, I would watch it. I yearned for someone to love me the way Noah loved Allie.

The scene that always gets me is when Allie finally received Noah's letters that he had written to her from her mother. She reads the last and final letter where Noah was saying goodbye. He writes to her (and it's one of my favorite quotes from the movie): "The best love is the kind that awakens the soul and makes us reach for more, that plants a fire in our hearts and brings peace to our minds, and that's what you've given me. That's what I hope to give you forever. I love you. I'll be seeing you." This was the kind of love I wanted in my life, and I wrote it down on a piece of paper and hung it on my vision board that I created. I engraved these words in my heart and told myself one day that I would find a guy who loves me this way. I was no longer going to give my body to men who were unavailable or in a committed relationship. I was going to change my karma and start taking care of my heart and soul. I affirmed out loud every day through positive quotes and affirmations. Sounds easy right? Well, it was easier said than done.

I was involved in a few more relationships that didn't work out, and I was over it all. I decided to try a dating app so I signed up for Tinder. For those who don't know about Tinder, it is a dating app that connects you with other people, but first, you both have to "swipe right." After you both swipe right, it becomes a match and you can then start chatting in the app. I heard mixed reviews from different people about Tinder, but I was going to have my own opinion about it. I matched with quite a few guys, but I didn't swipe right on all of them. I finally swiped right on someone and met what seemed like a nice guy named Bobby. We met in the spring of 2016 and started dating regularly. I guess you can say I was his girlfriend, even though sometimes it didn't feel that way. What was comforting and different about Bobby was that he actually was nice to me, but as we got further into the relationship, I wanted more. I affirmed to myself that I wasn't going to give up on love, but it was exhausting and I was pushing mid-40s. I thought that if I didn't find someone soon, I might as well just stay single for the rest of my life. So, I pressured Bobby to make a commitment to me. I know what you're thinking based on my history. Did she marry him too? Heck no, I didn't marry him! I just wanted a commitment from him.

Then, one day, while at the hair salon, I started talking to my hairdresser about how tired I was of dating and how my relationships were going nowhere. At least now I saw the red flags sooner and ended it faster instead of staying in a relationship that didn't serve me. In the hair salon, everyone can hear your conversations, and I didn't mind. It was like a bunch of girls getting together at a dinner party—only we weren't having dinner but having the same amount of fun. One of the hairdressers said to me, "You need to go see this psychic. She will tell you everything you need to know." At this point in my life, I was willing to try anything that would guide me. Have you ever tried doing something unfamiliar? I immediately thought, *I don't want to see a psychic. What if she tells me something about my future that I don't want to hear?* I had never seen a psychic in my life, and the fear of knowing what lay ahead scared me to death. But despite my fear, I decided to make an appointment.

The plan was to only see her one time, but I went into this experience with an open mind. I arrived at her place and I was expecting to go into an office-type setting, but it was her house. This scared me even more. What if this lady was crazy and kidnapped me? As I rang the doorbell, I was greeted by an older lady. My first impression of her was sweet, but she seemed guarded. I didn't know what to expect. At first, I thought she would take me into a dark room and have me lie down on a couch or something, but she invited me in and led me to a well-lit dining room with natural light. She asked me to sit down at the table, and we got to know each other for a little bit. Then she asked me, "So what do you want to know?" Geez, what a loaded question for a first-time psychic experience!

I said to her, "I don't know, but I guess I want to know if I will find the guy I am supposed to be with." She then proceeded to ask me what type of service did I want: a reading, crystal therapy, chakra clearing . . . So many options to choose from, and I didn't know what I wanted. I sensed she could see my nervousness, so she explained each service to me a bit more to help me decide. When she explained the chakra clearings, I was most interested in that, but I decided to do all three.

On my first visit, she did a reading for me. As she lay the cards down one by one in a horizontal row, she was already mentioning things about my life that were true. She said, "You are very driven and have a great career. You are motivated. You love your kids." Then she got to the religion card and paused, but she didn't say anything and kept going. Kind of odd, right? She proceeded to lay down more cards. She said, "You are with someone right now, but this is not the guy you will stay with. He cares about you, but he's not the one for you." How did she know this? By this time, I was already a believer of this psychic experience because so far everything she was saying was true. She went on to say, "The guy you will meet loves you unconditionally. He loves your boys and will take care of you like no other has. He is the man you will be with for the rest of your life." She was very specific when she said this next thing. "He has a daughter, and if you don't meet him by the end of 2017 or the beginning of 2018, you will never meet him."

Wow is right! I didn't know anyone with a daughter. I was speechless and wanted to ask more about this guy, but I felt guilty because I was dating someone currently. I was trying to change my karma, remember! So I didn't ask and let that one sit with me for a while. Gary, the love of my life, later told me that I was going to be the last girl he dated on Tinder because he was tired of the failed relationships and women not wanting to commit to him. This is probably what the psychic meant when she said if I didn't meet him by the end of 2017 or the beginning of 2018, I would never meet him.

I was new to chakra healing and asked the psychic to tell me how many chakras there were to help me make the right choice. She said, "There are seven chakras in the human body: Crown Chakra, Third Eye, Throat Chakra, Heart Chakra, Solar Plexus, Sacral Chakra, and Root Chakra." I really wanted to clear out all my chakras, but I chose the Heart Chakra to focus on. She gave me a piece of paper and told me to write these words down: "God is my father. Nature is my mother. Wisdom is my way. I see me now. Calm, quiet, and receptive. I see my heart peaceful and my mind tranquil. I see the ultraviolet light and the purple transmitting flame. Wisdom is within me now. I ask that I be placed in a white capsule of protection. And for this I give thanks."

She told me to say this prayer every night before bed, or at least two times per week. I would do ten minutes palms up saying the prayer out loud, five minutes palms down saying the prayer out loud, and five minutes palms down saying the prayer silently. I didn't understand any of this, but I trusted the process and came to it with an open mind. I did the prayer every night before bed.

I scheduled five more visits with the psychic. Her fees were too much for my budget, but I was able to commit to five more visits. I wanted to hear more about this mystery guy. I saw her before my 45th birthday trip to Mexico with Bobby. She told me to have fun and that she would see me when I got back. I probably shouldn't have gone on the trip since I was already feeling like things were not working out between me and Bobby, but he paid for everything and I needed a good vacation. Mexico was not an ideal vacation spot for me, but Bobby loved Mexico. I loved vacationing, however, and I would always make the best out of any situation, so I was excited to go.

As we were waiting to board the plane, I started getting a really bad stomachache. I had to rush to the restroom—it was that bad. I thought it was maybe something I ate, and I hoped the pain would be gone by the time we boarded the plane. Boy was I wrong! As soon as we boarded, I needed to go to the restroom again. I don't mean to be gross here, but I had the runs like there was no tomorrow. Having this issue on a plane is not fun. It was the worst stomachache I'd had in a very long time, and it was not a good start to our vacation.

Finally, we arrived in Mexico. I felt even worse as we deboarded the plane, and by the time we got to the hotel, I was running a slight fever. I was sicker than a dog. How could this be happening to me? I was on vacation, and it was my birthday. I tried my best to tough it out, but then the symptoms were persistent and getting worse. We went out for dinner and I could barely eat or drink anything. I was in tears at the dinner table. Bobby asked me what was wrong, and I told him, "I feel so sick but I don't want to ruin our trip." I don't recall what he said, but it was as cold as the food that was sitting on my uneaten plate. Bobby wasn't a mean guy—he just wasn't a warm and fuzzy kind of guy.

The next day I was majorly congested. My face looked like someone put a helium needle in me and added air. It was so puffy from being congested and my eyes felt like they were going to explode. We still ventured out into town to do some souvenir shopping and eat lunch. We found a place to eat, and by this time, I couldn't bear the sick feeling anymore. I said to Bobby, "What should I do?"

He said, "Go get some medicine. There is a drug store right there." All he cared about was ordering a drink. It was almost as if he was annoyed that I was sick. So, I mustered up what little energy that I had and headed to the nearby drug store. Everything was in Spanish on the package and I didn't understand anything. I asked the clerk if he had anything for feeling sick. I told him my symptoms and he gave me what was equivalent to Sudafed. He told me this was the best medicine and it would clear me up and make me feel better. I immediately took one and headed back to the restaurant. I still couldn't eat or drink anything, so I just sat there and watched Bobby enjoy his meal and drinks.

I don't know why I was so upset with Bobby. It was his vacation, too, and he was allowed to enjoy himself. I just wanted him to take care of me. Here I was, once again trying to make the person I was with love me the way I loved. Except I didn't love him, and he didn't love me. I realized that we never said "I love you" to each other. I was so used to guys saying I love you so quickly, but he never told me that. His behavior reaffirmed to me that he wasn't the guy I was supposed to be with—and you know what, I was ok with that. For the first time, I felt a sense of calm and peace in my mind and heart. Bobby wasn't a bad guy; he just wasn't the one for me.

As my birthday approached, Bobby had a nice day planned for us. The medicine had settled into my system and I was feeling a little better. Still congested but the fever and diarrhea were gone. Thank goodness! Bobby scheduled a spa day for the two of us. It was exactly what I needed, and it helped me feel better. When we arrived back to the room, the bed had *Happy 45th Birthday* written on it in bright-colored rice pieces and balloons everywhere. That night we had a nice dinner by the ocean. It was a very nice birthday, but I knew this was going to be the last trip Bobby and I took.

As soon as we arrived back home, Bobby and I stopped seeing each other. He told me exactly what I already knew. He said to me, "I can't love you the way you want me to." I said, "Well, then there is nothing more to say." We stopped seeing each other at the end of June 2017.

Not long after that, I made an appointment with my psychic and was excited to see her. This would be the last of my paid sessions. The first thing she asked me was, "How was your trip?"

I said, "I was really sick."

"That makes sense," she said. "You were clearing out your chakras and sometimes people get sick in the process." Bingo, the light bulb went on. I told her that Bobby and I decided not to continue with the relationship. This was my last session and I was really curious to know more about the mystery guy, so I asked her, "Can you tell me a little more about this guy I'm supposed to meet?"

She said, "Sure what do you want to know?"

"Do I know him?"

"No, you don't know him, and I can't tell you how you will meet him."

I left that last session feeling more confused than ever, so I let go of the thoughts of meeting this mystery guy. I released the thoughts out to the Universe and trusted the process.

It was fall, my favorite time of the year. Four months had gone by since my session with my psychic, and I became obsessed with meeting my mystery man. I stayed on Tinder and kept swiping right, hoping that the next guy would be the one the psychic told me about. I continued to meet the guys I matched with from the app, but the dates went nowhere. A lot of them wanted to have just a sexual relationship, and I was done with all of that, so I didn't give them a second chance to ask me out. I was finally getting stronger in my mind, body, and soul, and I was so proud of my progress. I was at a point in my life where not every guy I met was "the one." I didn't want to have relationships with guys who didn't check the boxes for me. Yes, I created a checklist of the man I wanted to spend the rest of my days and nights with. I knew he was out there, and I wasn't going to give up on love. I knew I deserved it and was worthy of everything I wanted in life. I even started dating myself!

As part of my self-love journey and discovering what I love to do, one of my therapists told me to get out there and do things by myself. She told me that being alone was a great opportunity to be in the present moment and open my mind up to make more conscious decisions. I decided to take myself on a mini weekend getaway to a small town that I loved going to: Sausalito, California. It was a weekend I didn't have my boys, so it was the perfect time to get away. I booked a four-star boutique hotel for one night, and in the package, there was an option to add a cheese platter with a bottle of wine that would be waiting when I arrived at the hotel, and I added this to the reservation. When I arrived at the hotel, I felt like a princess in a castle. I had a balcony that overlooked the marina, and the room was nice with a fireplace. I ordered room service so that I could just relax and enjoy the peaceful moment. When I was done with dinner, I ventured out to the marina where I could watch the sunset, but before I did this, I stopped to get the best ice cream in town to take with me.

Sunsets always make me feel happy inside. They make me feel peaceful and give me a strong sense of gratitude for life. When I lived by the beach, I would watch the sunset almost every night for a year. I would stop on the side of a road just to take pictures if I saw a beautiful sunset. Sunsets heal my soul. I have seen many beautiful sunsets, but this one was by far the most beautiful I have ever seen. In this moment of peace, my heart was whole and free of pain. The next day before I left for home, I went shopping in town and bought myself a few nice things. I didn't want to go home and wanted to stay in this feeling of bliss forever.

Self-Love Lesson

"I open my heart and sing the joys of love."

- Louise Hay

14

I Love You Mostest, Second

"When you meet the other half of your soul you'll understand why it didn't work out with anyone else."

- Unknown

I didn't check Tinder the entire time I was in Sausalito, so when I got home, I jumped on the app. I started doing the usual, swiping and reading the profiles in my feed. I was swiping left on a lot of the profiles until I got to one particular one. His name was Gary, and based on his profile, he wanted a lot of the same things I wanted: a serious relationship with someone he could have fun with and enjoy life. He had kids like me, and guess what? He had a daughter. I thought to myself, could he be the one the psychic was talking about? He was handsome, and his picture looked friendly, so I swiped right. Gary's picture popped up, which meant that he had swiped right also.

At this point, we were able to start chatting with each other. He must have been online because he immediately started chatting with me. To stay safe and make sure these guys were who they said they were, I chatted through the app before giving them my number.

After chatting with Gary a few times back and forth, I felt comfortable giving him my contact information. We exchanged numbers and the rest is history. Yeah, right! You see, Gary was coming into my life after three failed marriages and multiple failed relationships. Trust had to be earned, and I wasn't the girl who was going to let just any guy into my life so easily anymore. If you ask me, he should have run for the hills. Just kidding! I had a lot of love to give but I was protecting my heart like gold.

We talked for weeks before I finally agreed to meet him for our first date. Between the schedule with my boys and his work schedule, it was a little challenging to get on each other's calendars, but we made it work. Our first date was in November 2017. So far the psychic was right. Gary had a daughter, and I met him before the end of 2017. I still had my doubts, however, and I promised myself that I would take every relationship at my pace and not be rushed into anything that I didn't want to do. At this point, I felt comfortable enough to meet him at his place so that we could take one car. I also wanted to meet his daughter. He was so excited to meet me that he walked up to my car and opened my door for me. He had on a bright orange cowboy-looking button-up shirt with some nice jeans and orange shoes to match his shirt. I felt underdressed, but he assured me that I wasn't. He complimented me very respectfully and nicely. His daughter was adorable and very sweet. So far, we were off to a good start for a first date!

I told him that I liked wine tasting, so he picked out a few nice wineries in town for us to visit. We visited wineries I had never been to but had always wanted to try. We arrived at the first winery, and Gary was gushing with so much to share. I already could see the sparkle in his eyes. The way he looked at me was different than the other guys. He didn't look at me like I was just a piece of meat that he would devour at the end of the night. His eyes were not only beautiful, they were sweet and gentle. He looked and talked to me with so much respect and admiration. It was almost unreal. I was so used to men skipping the getting-to-know-you part and shoving their tongues down my throat. Not Gary. He wanted to know everything about me. He truly was the sweetest man I had ever laid eyes on.

I don't know what it was, but he made me feel comfortable. We laughed, shared stories of our lives and our children. I found out he had not only one daughter but two, and a son also. He was married previously but only once. His mindset was like mine, and that he told himself he would never marry again. Apparently, he had a bad experience with his ex-wife. He didn't run or end the date when I told him that I had four boys and had been married twice. I was too ashamed to tell him about the third marriage, so I withheld that piece about my life. It was a time of my life that I was never going to share with anyone. I wanted that time to disappear, but I knew that he would eventually need to know. Little did I know that one day, the story would be in a book!

Our date was coming to an end, and we were heading back to his place so that I could pick up my car. I had a bit too much wine and needed to rest a bit before hitting the road. He offered to let me stay with him until I sobered up. We were both attracted to each other, and not just on a physical level. It felt different this time. We connected on an emotional level. I knew what would happen if I went inside, and against all my will, I went in. Of course, I could have just sat down on a chair, but I chose the bed and really needed to lay down. Wine tasting always relaxed me and was a good sleep remedy. I wanted to take a nap, so I asked him if he wanted to take a nap with me. Without hesitation, he said, "Yes, of course." But we didn't just take a nap. He made love to me like no other man has in my life, and it was magical. I wanted to spend the night, but I was already disappointed in myself for sleeping with him on the first date. I had a fear that because the intimacy started right away, he wouldn't want me anymore. I was completely wrong. He continued to call me, and our relationship blossomed into something I never could have imagined.

As much as I wanted to believe that Gary was falling in love with me, I kept my guard up. I protected my heart and made him work for my love. I learned my lesson from the past, and I wasn't going to give my heart to just anyone anymore. Every morning I woke up to a love letter from Gary in my email, and he never let me start the day without calling me to say good morning. He even set his alarm clock to make sure he talked to me before I left for work. You see, Gary wasn't a morning person and I was. He worked late nights and I worked early mornings. Our schedules were completely opposite, but that didn't stop him from accommodating me. I remember the first love letter he wrote me. It was the most heartfelt and sincere letter. As I read it, my future flashed in front of me, and he was by my side every step of the way. I felt like Allie from *The Notebook*, and Gary was my Noah. I told myself, *I think I found the love that I was searching for all my life.*

The difference was, my heart was free and open to receive the love I deserved. I finally attracted a guy who loved me for who I was and didn't try to make me someone I am not. There is a beautiful quote, "We've lost a lot of years, but you can't lose love. Not real love. It stays locked inside you, ready for whenever you are strong enough to find it again."

I kept the letter and wanted to share it here:

I just wanted to write you a letter to let you know some things. I am so blessed to have you in my life now and am thankful for meeting such an amazing woman!! I can truly say that I have NEVER had a woman make me feel the way you make me feel mentally and physically. I wake up and go to bed every single day as the happiest man because of you and think about you all day and night. I know that deep in my heart and the strongest gut feeling I have ever had in my life that you are my PERFECT match. You warm my heart every day and make me smile more than I have ever before. I want nothing more than to be your BEST friend and LOVER forever!!!!!! I want to make new friends together with you and to create our love as one and never want to spend another day without you in my life. I can't wait to meet your beautiful family and for you to meet mine and to begin our new life together. I LOVE YOU LORRINE.

Gary and I dated for six months before I told him that I loved him. I wanted to be sure that I loved him, and he loved me. We have this funny saying, even today. When we say I love you to each other, he will always say, "I love you mostest, first." And I say, "I love you mostest, second." We got along so well that sometimes I would purposely pick fights with him because that's what I was used to. I was used to chaos and yelling, and when he didn't fight back and feed into my insecurities that still lingered, I realized what I was doing and stopped picking fights. This man wasn't going anywhere, and this was definitely something I had to get used to. I was unconsciously putting him through a series of tests, and he was passing each one with flying colors.

I still had a hard time trusting, and I would oftentimes ask him questions about his Facebook and Instagram followers if I saw girls on there. He would comfort me and tell me that I had nothing to worry about. Even though I didn't ask for this, he gave me his passwords to his phone, email, and social media. He wanted me to feel safe and trust him. He would tell me multiple times that he was with me and I was the only person he wanted to be with forever. This was something else I wasn't used to. I expected him to yell at me and tell me that I was causing trouble and that I needed psychiatric help because this is what other guys have told me in the past. He was everything those guys weren't—a patient, caring gentlemen who wanted to take care of me and my boys and who always had our best interests in his heart. He loved me unconditionally, for all my imperfections and flaws. The more time we spent together, the closer we got and the more I trusted him with my heart.

I wanted to be honest with Gary, and I knew that the time had come to tell him about Leon and the kind of relationship we had. I didn't want him to find out years later—and good thing I told him, because he would have heard about it in this book that I was manifesting. We were in a Safeway parking lot about to go into the store when I said, "I have to tell you something."

My heart was pounding so hard it felt like it was going to pop out of my chest and start running. I took a few deep breaths, but I couldn't hold back the tears that started to well up in my eyes. I started to tell him about my relationship with Leon and that we eventually married, but after discovering that he had a cuckold fantasy and wanted me to be a part of it, I divorced him. I couldn't even finish explaining to him all the reasons why I didn't stay in that marriage. At this point, I was crying so hard because of all the shame and hurt I had carried for so long alone. Gary was the first person I shared this with. I knew for sure he was not going to want to be with me now, but it was the complete opposite of what I expected. He held me tight, wiped my tears away, and said to me, "I love you for who you are. It doesn't matter what is in your past. We all have done things in the past that we regret, but we need to move forward and not worry about the past." In this moment, I knew Gary was my soulmate and the man I would spend the rest of my life with.

Gary's niece invited us to her wedding in Utah in June 2018. This would be the first time I would meet his family and I was extremely nervous. What if they didn't like me? I purchased a beautiful dress and frantically started searching for someone to do my hair and makeup in Utah for the wedding. Yes, I was taking this meeting of the family way too seriously, but I wanted to make a good first impression. The week prior I had a work trip scheduled, and I planned on meeting Gary and my boys in Utah. I was exhausted and tired from my work trip when I arrived at the Salt Lake International Airport. I didn't know where I was going and needed directions on how to get to the hotel where Gary and my boys were. I called him but got no answer. I left a voicemail and texted him. After ten minutes of no response, I called him again. No answer. I was getting worried at this point and starting to panic. I was at an unfamiliar place and I didn't know where to go. Finally, after twenty minutes, Gary called me back. I was in tears by then and was really upset with him for not answering his phone. He spoiled me so much that

I wasn't used to him not answering my calls or texts. I was also very exhausted, so my emotions were on high alert.

I finally arrived at the hotel and Gary greeted me at the car to help with my luggage. I was so happy to see him and my boys. As soon as we got to the room, Gary told me he would be right back. I was still so full of emotion from the airport experience that I immediately got upset. Why didn't he want to spend time with me? I hadn't seen him for over a week and he would rather spend time with other people? I took a shower and went to lie down. After about forty-five minutes, I called him to see where he was. He told me he was on his way back. By the time he got back to the room, I was furious and just laid into him. I started to raise my voice, "First you didn't answer your phone, and now you didn't want to spend time with me!" I knew I was being a royal pain in the ass, but I wanted to be heard.

He said, "I'm sorry babe, I was with my family and didn't see you texting or calling me." I realized that I was overreacting and I apologized to him for getting upset. I said to him, "I just missed you and was excited to spend time together." Gary and I made ourselves a promise that we would never go to bed angry or upset. We both apologized to each other, kissed, and made up.

The next day was the wedding, and I was going to meet his family for the first time. By this time, my nerves were gone. I knew they would love me because I loved Gary. And I was right. His family welcomed me with open arms and his dad was the sweetest man I'd ever met. No wonder Gary was so sweet. His dad was the same way as him. The wedding was in a beautiful setting and absolutely amazing. In a few days, it would be my birthday, and it didn't matter if I got presents or not. I had the best presents a girl could ever ask for. I finally found the love of my life—I was healthy, I had amazing kids, and most of all, I found the peace in my heart that I was searching for all my life. Turning forty-six was the day my life would change forever. Gary was secretly planning a surprise for me, and boy, was I going to be surprised.

On the day before my birthday, I woke up thinking to myself, *Gosh, I am in my late forties and approaching my fifties. I never thought this day would come because I almost took my life and didn't think I would make it past fifty.* I looked and felt better than I ever have in my life. Gary was extra excited on this day. It was as if it was almost *his* birthday. He said, "The family wants to meet for breakfast and take some family pictures after." It was a beautiful, sunny, warm day. We met his family for breakfast and afterward all walked to the courtyard where there was a beautiful water feature. As we all stood around, Gary said to me, "Let's go take our picture first."

I said, "Why do we have to go first?"

I didn't want to go and was so embarrassed. There were so many family members around and we would be in the spotlight taking pictures by ourselves. I think Gary's niece could sense my fear, so she came over to us and said, "Come on, we will come take the pictures with you." As we got up to the water feature, his niece and her new husband left the group. Then Gary started to talk. He said, "Are we ready?" and pulled me towards him to take a picture. I was so confused and not sure why all these people were staring at us when it was supposed to be a group family picture. Then Gary turned to his family and said, "You guys know that I love this woman and she means the world to me." Then he got down on one knee, opened a small blue box with a beautiful ring, and said, "Lorrine, you are the love of my life, and I want nothing but to spend the rest of my life with you. Will you marry me?" I didn't even think about an answer and immediately said, "Yes!" It was truly the most romantic wedding proposal, and I later found out that everyone was in on the surprise except for me. This is what he was doing the night I arrived, and I felt so horrible for getting so upset with him! I know what you're thinking, is this marriage going to last? Trust me, when I said "I do," I thought the same thing, but that thought was based on fear, and this time, fear wasn't going to win. My mind, body, and soul were at a place where fear wasn't a part of my life anymore. I chose love and love chose me.

Self-Love Lesson

"Something inside you emerges, an innate, indwelling peace, stillness, aliveness. It is the unconditioned, who you are in your essence. It is what you had been looking for in the love object. It is yourself."

- Echhart Tolle

15

Happily Ever After

"Being deeply loved by someone gives you strength,
while loving someone deeply give you courage."

- Lao Tzu

We chose a wedding date of August 9, 2019, because we both felt this date flowed well together just like our love. It was perfect in every way, shape, and form. Planning this wedding was completely different than my other weddings because Gary was by my side every step of the way. This marriage would be like no other, and it was special to both of us. He wanted to be part of the entire planning from start to finish. It was truly like a fairy tale, a dream come true. We both wanted to marry on or near the water, so Gary had an amazing idea to marry on a yacht. I loved the idea and started searching for the perfect yacht that would hold one hundred people, which was the guest count we both decided on. I searched high and low for weddings on a yacht, and I came across a place called Commodore Cruises and Events in a nearby city called Alameda. This venue was perfect for our wedding size, and the package was all-inclusive and included the dessert, food, drinks, yacht, flowers, and the captain to marry us. We would be directly on the water like we wanted for the wedding ceremony, and then we'd sail the bay for our reception with dinner and dancing. A big reason why we selected this venue is each yacht had the name of a wine, which reminded us of our perfect first date at the wineries. We booked the venue and chose to marry on The Merlot. I wanted the Pinot Noir, my favorite red wine, but this yacht was a lot bigger and way out of our budget. I was happy with The Merlot because it didn't matter where I married Gary as long as I had him by my side saying, "I do."

The wedding dress shopping went rather well, and I asked my daughter-in-law to join me. I didn't want to go to several stores, so I chose one and made sure that my wedding dress would be at this store. I also knew my budget, and I didn't want to spend more than $1,000 for a dress that I would only wear once. I wanted to look beautiful for Gary but I didn't need to spend thousands of dollars. When I told the store attendant how much my budget was, she looked at me in an awkward way and told me that with this budget there wasn't going to be much selection. Apparently, these employees worked off commission and her commission wasn't going to be large with my purchase. She brought me five dresses, all of which I tried on. Of course, they were smaller than me and I had to squeeze my boobs and butt into them. I finally came to one I fell in love with. It was comfortable, stretchy, showed a little skin (which I knew Gary would like), and it was off white. It was the most perfect dress. We decided not to have a traditional large wedding party, so we asked our children to walk down the aisle with each other. We paired them up in twos and threes. My grandson Mason was the ring bearer, and Jescey, Gary's daughter, was the flower girl. It was very important to both me and Gary that our kids were part of the wedding ceremony. Our families were blending together as one, and we wanted them to be part of this special day.

Gary and I finished the planning within three months of being engaged. It was amazing that now we could just enjoy each other's company and get used to the idea of being around each other 24/7. By this time, Gary was spending every night at my place and had practically moved in already. We enjoyed a lot of the same things and had the best time with everything we did together. We made a commitment to each other to always have a date night, and we chose the 5th of every month because that is when we had our first date. At first, we tried different places, but then we fell in love with a place called Haberdasher. A co-worker mentioned it to me and highly recommended it. It was a small speakeasy type cocktail bar where you could reserve a table and get personalized service. The staff was all dressed as tailors and the way I understood it is that you tell them what you like to drink and they make a drink for you. If you didn't like the drink after trying it, they would take it back and tailor it to your liking. It was so romantic with dim lighting, music, red walls, and huge red velvet curtains hanging everywhere. We even made friends with a bartender we connected with and invited him to our wedding. It was our special place, and we loved it here.

One night while enjoying our date night, I felt kind of strange. It was a feeling that I'd had before, so I said to Gary, "I don't feel well, can we go?" The familiar feeling was coming on fast this time and I told Gary that I had to go to the restroom. As I bolted to the restroom, the last thing I remember is pushing the door open. I woke up on the ground of the dirty restroom floor. I was lying on my back, my phone and belongings from my hand spread out under the stall nearby. My head was pounding, and my right arm had a sharp pain. A girl was standing over me asking me if I was okay. She started to hand me my belongings that were all over the place. I was completely out of sorts and had no idea what just happened. I thought, did I drink too much? I only had two drinks. It couldn't have been that. I managed to pick myself up and go into the restroom stall to call Gary. I was sweating profusely and was so embarrassed that this happened in public. After about ten minutes, I was able to walk and leave the restroom. I saw Gary waiting for me. He asked me, "What happened to you?" I told him, "I don't know. I guess I passed out." I had a huge knot on the back of my head and my right arm was throbbing in pain. I like to say my Guardian Angel was looking out for me because it could have been a lot worse. It was as if someone caught me and laid me down on the floor. I landed perfectly between a pedestal sink and the restroom stalls.

The next day I went to the doctor and got scolded for not going to the emergency room the night I passed out. The doctor told me that what happened to me was not normal. I told him that this had happened to me once before at a nail salon getting a pedicure. You could see the confusion on his face. He ordered some tests for me to get done and every test came back normal, except one of the tests showed signs of anemia. It was still a mystery as to what happened to me, so he advised me to go see my OBGYN after I told him my menstrual cycles were abnormal. I had to change my super plus tampon and overnight pad every thirty minutes for a day when I was on my period. He thought maybe this had something to do with the fainting and why I was showing as being anemic. I scheduled an appointment with my OBGYN immediately. I too wanted to find out what was wrong with me and why I fainted the way I did. It kind of all made sense to me because on the night I fainted, I was on my period and bleeding profusely.

My diagnosis was that I had a condition called endometriosis and would need a hysterectomy. Thank goodness I wasn't going to have more kids, but I still felt a little bit of sadness getting it removed. I felt like my womanhood was being stripped from me, but I knew that it was for the best. My surgery was scheduled for March 2019. I wanted to get this done before Gary and I got married so that we could enjoy the wedding and our honeymoon. Gary was by my side the entire time from when I was brought into surgery to my recovery in the hospital. He never left my side. For the first time in my life, all of my insecurities and trust issues dissipated, and I knew that Gary was my one true soul mate and the love of my life. I still think back to this time and get teary-eyed because no one has ever taken care of me the way Gary does. There have even been nights when I would drink too much and he would change me into my pajamas and put me to bed. One night I had over fifty bobby pins in my hair that he removed for me one by one.

For the last three years, I haven't had to cook dinner because Gary cooks for us almost every night. He waters my flowers and massages my back every night. He cares for the boys like his own. He has the most patience of anyone I know. He does everything for me. There are many qualities that I love about Gary, but most of all, I love him for his kind, loving heart. I asked the Universe for twenty-nine years to bring me Gary, and it wasn't until I found self-love and dated myself that I knew what it was like to be treated well. I now know what it feels like to be truly loved. We got married in August 2019, and it was the most perfect wedding anyone could ask for. Surrounded by our children, family, and friends, we said "I do."

For the first time, I wasn't settling or marrying someone to fulfill a void in my life. Gary and I were adding to each other lives, and today we are the happiest we have ever been. There's a beautiful quote I love, "There is no such thing as the 'perfect' man or woman. Just find one who tries hard enough to make you happy and wants to grow with you." No relationship is perfect, including ours, but with communication, honesty, understanding, patience, and love, you can get through anything.

I am not going to tell you that my life is perfect and that I don't still experience sadness, because that wouldn't be true. The truth is that writing this book has brought me the inner healing that I needed to forgive myself and others. I didn't know that I was still carrying a lot of the pain from my past, and thought I was healed. Boy was I wrong! There is a quote I love by David Pelzer that speaks to me: "When we forgive, we free ourselves from the bitter ties that bind us from the one who hurt us." I had a lot of buried emotions that surfaced throughout the writing of this book, but the difference is, I knew how to handle it. I am much stronger in my mind, body, and soul because of it.

Some people live their entire lives not knowing what true love and happiness feels like. You don't have to be that person. Through the power of positive thinking, affirmations, and visualizing what you want in life, you can find what you are truly seeking in your mind, body, and soul. I found my true happiness, purpose, and passion, but most of all, I found myself and the ability to love with an open heart and mind. I hope that through my experiences, you are encouraged and inspired to overcome the difficult challenges that have happened in your life. It will take hard work, determination, and willpower to get there, but you will. If I could leave you with one final thought, it would be to never give up and continue to love yourself because you are always enough. You are always loved.

"Purpose is an essential element. The struggles that I had along the way were meant to shape me for my purpose."

- Chadwick Brosnick

My Secret Love Symbol – Hummingbird

When I was going through a difficult situation at work, I decided to start listening to an audiobook called *The Power* by Rhonda Byrne. I already read about her first book *The Secret*, so I had a strong feeling that *The Power* would guide me through this tough time. Every morning on my way to work, I would listen to *The Power*. I got to a chapter called "The Power and You." There was a part in this chapter that stuck with me called "Your Secret Symbol." In this part of the book, Rhonda talks about playing with the law of attraction by asking to see physical evidence of the force of love. You see, my difficult situation was having to deal with someone who showed no love and had a hard exterior shell. I knew I was never going to change her, nor did I want to change her. I knew that I could only change my thinking towards her. Rhonda says "Think of something you love, and make it your symbol of the force of love. Whenever you see your symbol or hear it, you will know that the force of love is with you." After I heard this, my immediate visualization was a hummingbird. I have always loved hummingbirds. I even got a tattoo of one in 1988. I knew it was my perfect symbol. I called it my love symbol. When I arrived home, and to my surprise, hummingbirds were on my back patio feeding from our hummingbird feeder. Over the next few weeks and months, they were there almost every day. We would go places and see hummingbirds. They were everywhere. I felt so much love inside, and when I would arrive at work, the unloving person was the same person but this time it didn't bother me. I prayed for her happiness instead and hoped that one day she would find her secret symbol.

Acknowledgments

To my amazing and wonderful husband, Gary. I couldn't have written this book without your support, patience, and love. Thank you for always stopping what you were doing to listen to an idea I had or hear each line I wrote in the book. Thank you for holding me up and wiping my tears when I had to write about the tough parts. You never let me give up and encouraged me to keep going. This book would not be what it is without you by my side. I love you mostest, second!

To my loving and understanding children. When I mentioned to you all that I was writing a book, I received nothing but support and love. I am beyond blessed to have such wonderful children and I am thankful that I get to be your mom. Hopefully this book will provide some clarity as to what I went through in my life and how much I have grown to be the mother I was meant to be. My life would not be whole without all of you in it. I love you to the moon and back!

Laurel Braitman hosted a virtual workshop in April 2020 and I didn't know this workshop would change my life forever. What started as a fun idea turned into writing a book. Thank you, Laurel, for being my book angel and guiding me towards my journey of writing a book. I will be forever grateful.

I am thankful for meeting many amazing new friends along the way. I am especially thankful for my visionary warrior sisters, Suzanne and Joh. We were brought together by fate and are now sisters for life. Your friendship and support throughout the book-writing process will never be forgotten. Thank you for the laughs and positivity that you both brought into my life. I love you, my forever sisters.

Finding an editor was one of the most challenging things in the process. I wanted to make sure that I found an editor that would vibe well with me. When I found Keith Gordon on Fiverr, it was truly a blessing in disguise. I pulled an Angel card and asked to show me a hummingbird or bird to let me know that I should go with Keith as my editor. The card was the Knight of Air and had a bird. Keith was exactly the editor that I needed to bring my book to life. Thank you, Keith, for your amazing expertise and guidance. You made the editing process smooth and stress-free. You can find him at duostorytelling.com.

Last but not least, I am thankful for my Buddhist member family, the writing community, and my amazing new friends and supporters on Instagram, Facebook, and Twitter. You all believed in me and my story before it was finished, and I want to thank you from the bottom of my heart. I am blessed to have each of you in my life.